this fragile life

this fragile life

a mother's story of a bipolar son

CHARLOTTE PIERCE-BAKER

Lawrence Hill Books

Chicago

Copyright © 2012 by Charlotte Pierce-Baker
Poetry and prose excerpts copyright © 2012 by Mark Frederick Baker
All rights reserved
First edition
Published by Lawrence Hill Books
An imprint of Chicago Review Press, Incorporated
814 North Franklin Street
Chicago, Illinois 60610
ISBN 978-1-61374-108-5

To ensure privacy, many names have been changed.

Library of Congress Cataloging-in-Publication Data
Pierce-Baker, Charlotte.
  This fragile life : a mother's story of a bipolar son / Charlotte
Pierce-Baker. — 1st ed.
    p. cm.
  Includes bibliographical references and index.
  ISBN 978-1-61374-108-5 (hardcover)
 1. Manic-depressive persons—United States—Biography.
 2. Manic-depressive persons—Family relationships—United States.
 3. African Americans—Mental health. I. Title.
  RC516.P58 2012
  616.89'50092—dc23
  [B]
                                        2011050228

Interior design: PerfecType, Nashville, TN

Printed in the United States of America
5 4 3 2 1

For Mark
Who trusted me to tell his story

contents

four

preface

IN THE SUMMER OF 1996, our son, Mark, made his cri de coeur from Los Angeles. My husband and I were thousands of miles away in Philadelphia, Pennsylvania. Mark was twenty-five years old, living with his fiancée, Lisa, and pursuing an advanced degree in film studies at the University of Southern California. Earlier that evening, when he could not find us by telephone, Mark had called Washington, DC, to speak with my father, who, in turn, called us. My father described Mark as being in "some sort of trouble. Mark was saying strange things and would not stop talking." He told us to wait for Mark's call.

When I answered the phone a few hours later, I heard the panic in my son's voice. In guarded tones, he whispered, "Mom, they're watching me. I can see them all around. They're watching me. I don't know what to do. Help me, Mom!" There were tears just beyond his words. His voice sounded hurried, fearful, tight; I felt his agitation. I almost believed he was being watched.

My husband and I desperately tried to figure out what was happening with our only son. Was he in physical danger? Was he having a nervous breakdown? His need for rescue was clear. Talking to him in turns, we attempted to convey some degree of calm. We assured Mark that his father would catch the next plane to Los Angeles to bring him home to Philadelphia. I would be at home, waiting.

In my absolute naïveté, I believed that Mark simply needed a few weeks to regroup from the stress of graduate school. In reality, our son was experiencing his first psychotic episode, and he would later be diagnosed with Bipolar Disorder Type I. We had been blindsided. Thousands of miles away, Mark had progressed brilliantly yet sleeplessly through his graduate courses at USC. Amidst his studies, he lost his bearings. He heard voices from Neptune speaking of cosmic designs, which competed regularly with the wisdom of his professors. Mark was gaunt, messianic, in touch with planets and whole worlds of delusion unknown to us. In real time, he would come to meet the rough, cold, metallic life of city jails and hospital gurneys, the suffering of an "unquiet mind," to borrow Kay Redfield Jamison's phrase.

There are few published accounts of families dealing with bipolar disorder; still fewer are written from a mother's perspective. *This Fragile Life* is the story of an upper-middle-class, African American family facing the challenges of mental illness. Our son, Mark, is a graduate of Germantown Friends, a Quaker preparatory school, in Philadelphia, the recipient of a bachelor's degree from the University of Pennsylvania and a master's degree from the University of Southern California. I was not naïve enough to think these privileges guaranteed exemption from illness, accident, disability, or even death. Looking back, however, I realize I had once assumed that giving Mark the best education available would enable him to do whatever he wanted in life and to succeed. As his mother, I never could have imagined he would wind up handcuffed, barely clothed, dirty, mad, and in jail. When Mark's first psychotic episode occurred, my real education began.

The horror of what was happening to Mark was compounded by our family's ignorance; we knew nothing of mental illness except what we had viewed in films or read in newspapers and novels. The images of mental illness in popular culture are exaggerated and meant to shock; in them, we saw no resemblance to our son. We were not in close proximity to Mark's adult life and had not been near enough geographically to witness his day-to-day behavior. He had not lived with us since leaving for college at the age of eighteen.

When Mark crashed, we attempted to piece together the previous months and years of his life. We discovered he had been bouncing from depression to hypomania, back to depression and then to full mania, often combined with bouts of paranoia and psychosis. We also learned that for many years, the exact number yet to be determined, he had tried to quiet his demons with drugs and alcohol. I learned that the name of this double affliction, which combines both mental illness and substance addiction, is *dual diagnosis*. Gradually, Mark descended into madness and then hit rock bottom.

Our nightmare existence commenced: hospitalizations, calls in the night, pleas for money and more money, jail (more times than we could admit to ourselves), lawyers, prescriptions (when we were lucky), doctors, drug and alcohol relapses (yet again), and continuous disputes about how to live and how not to live in order to remain well. Mark's journey toward recovery has been long, arduous, and nearly fatal. At this point, it seems an eternity.

Our son, Mark, is a dedicated poet. The music of words has always fascinated him; he began writing verses when he was nine years old. Throughout his years of illness, poetry has been tethered to the emotional currents of his daily life. Mark and I decided to include some of his poetry and prose throughout *This Fragile Life*, in particular his post-psychotic explanations and self-revelations. He writes eloquently of becoming a father while suffering from depression and mania, high on drugs and alcohol. In haunted words, Mark gives voice to the melancholy of his lost life:

> *Oh what I wouldn't give*
> *to have it all back again*
> *the way we lived*
> *and how the city lights*
> *drowned out the sin*
> *eager to see those freeways*

weave in and out for miles
while listening to Friday night DJs
spin their hard core styles.
So enchanted . . .
I took this fragile life for granted.

My husband and I awake each day with gratitude for our son's willingness to meet the challenges that bipolar disorder brings. At times, I am still fearful; I feel vulnerable and alone. Our son must take care of his illness, day by day, for the rest of his life. There is no cure. Bipolar is forever.

this fragile life

one

early and middle years

MARK WAS A GORGEOUS NEWBORN. Everyone thought so: our friends, his grandparents, his aunts and uncles—even our next-door neighbors. He was a C-section baby and had not one wrinkle on his smooth brown body. Only a frown creased his brow, as if he had a premonition of his future. Mark was a quiet, amiable baby, easily amused that winter of 1971. My husband and I loved to exchange Mark stories at the end of a day. "You'll *never* guess what he did today!" I would say. Small baby miracles, cooing or reaching for dangling earrings, comprised our love-struck conversations during Mark's first year. Friends who had not yet started families took delight in the development of our son. During Mark's early years, my days were dedicated only to him; I was a stay-at-home mom. If I close my eyes and conjure up that time, I can still see Mark's broad, toothless grin as I nuzzled his tummy with kisses while changing his diaper. His belly laughs, when he was really tickled, made me smile at the sound of sheer joy. Since Houston was a university professor with a flexible schedule, he and I took turns with Mark's diaper changes and stroller walks. In fact, Mark delighted in his father's bathing rituals. There were continuous splashes and giggles amidst Houston's imitated animal sounds, which accompanied his fantasy stories at bath time.

Toward the end of his first year, our wonderful, happy baby, for no apparent reason, began to have night terrors. Out of a deep sleep he would begin to whimper, then cry and scream with his eyes wide open. Running into his room with Houston at my heels, I realized that Mark was still asleep but in severe distress. With trial and error, we found that gently calling his name and rocking him

[5]

under bright lights soothed him into wakefulness. We learned to wait for the big smile to overtake his face, and then all was right again. Mark seemed to have no memory of the previous shattering moments; he was quick to be comforted. When we mentioned this to our pediatrician, he assured us that many babies had these random unaccounted-for occurrences. I told myself that Mark was having delayed separation anxiety because he'd had to leave the security of the womb. A silly explanation, but it appeased me.

In Charlottesville, Virginia, his birthplace, Mark continued his mostly easygoing babyhood. Charlottesville is a small town with an exquisitely beautiful university campus nestled at the foothills of the Blue Ridge Mountains. Nevertheless, in the early 1970s, this idyllic southern town remained predominately white. Friends and family suggested that opportunities for a growing African American child would be greater elsewhere, but Houston and I decided to remain a few more years where we were. We were content.

Then an unexpected incident happened when Mark was almost three. He was refused admission to a highly recommended daycare center. By telephone, the daycare center director told me there was "definitely a vacancy" for our son at her facility in town, adding, "We certainly need more boys!" I made an appointment for the next day.

When Mark and I arrived at the daycare center, it was naptime. The director peered through the screen door, looked me over, and then told me I was mistaken about having an appointment. In a clipped, pseudo-businesslike tone, she said there were no vacancies, that enrollment for the fall was complete. "But yesterday you told me you needed more boys," I said. I asked her to let us in since she had not opened the door in any gesture of welcome. Grudgingly, she complied.

Children were getting out their blankets and sleeping bags, and Mark began to wiggle excitedly when he saw the other children.

Looking around the room filled entirely with white children, I asked her, "By the way, do you have any black children enrolled?"

At my inquiry, the director began to blink uncomfortably and replied in a whispered voice, "It's not me, you understand. I have no problem. It's what my other mothers would say if I let you in."

I felt like I had been slapped. I quickly replied, "It *is* your problem." Livid, trying to make my way to the door, stumbling over cots and sleeping bags, I pulled Mark away from the toys and preschoolers, saying sternly, "We have to go now."

Not wanting to leave, Mark began to scream like a headstrong toddler torn away from fun. "No, no, no!" he yelled, tears streaming.

The director put out her hands to console him; I snatched Mark out of her reach and with clenched teeth warned, "Do not touch my son!"

I barely made it out the door before tears blinded me. Mark continued to sniffle while we were in the car, and I promised we would find another playgroup. "This one is already full of children, sweetheart," I explained. "No more can get in." I cried quietly all the way home.

Houston and I were devastated. Mark could not possibly understand racial differences and their complications; we wondered why children, so early, had to suffer the problems of grown-ups. We made phone calls to neighbors and other parents to report the preschool encounter. They were appalled that race discrimination could happen in a university community. But a few days later, I overheard a departmental secretary at the university whisper loudly to another worker, "There *are* daycare centers for blacks in town." We reported the incident to local newspapers, but nothing came of it except a few embarrassed phone calls from other daycare centers offering to welcome our son.

Much later, when Mark became ill with bipolar disorder, his identity as an African American man would become the focus of his self-doubt, alienation, and, ultimately, his paranoia. At the time of the daycare incident, our family knew nothing about what the future would bring; we hoped he would never face this kind of prejudice again.

After experiencing daycare discrimination, I decided to set up playdates in our home for some of the children of other mothers associated with the university. They had also faced similar daycare problems. Four of us formed a playgroup. We exchanged days and rotated on and off as babysitters so that each of us would have time alone for errands, knowing our children were cared for.

Shortly thereafter, Houston and I left Charlottesville for Philadelphia, Pennsylvania. Mark was three and a half. In an urban center, we hoped there would be a better choice of schools for Mark and a range of playmates in mixed-race neighborhoods. Houston accepted a professorship in the English department at the University of Pennsylvania, and I enrolled in graduate school at Temple University. The three of us settled into our row house just west of the center of town. The only difficulty Mark seemed to have was learning to walk in sneakers on concrete. In Charlottesville, he had preferred bare feet; the house was surrounded by grass.

We had lived in Philadelphia for about a year when Mark began to sleepwalk. Still asleep, with no distress and with his eyes open, he would walk right by us, saying he was "going bowling" or "going to visit my friend." His wanderings led us to put an inside security lock on the front door, lest we lose our child to the night. Since no how-to manual accompanies birthing and child rearing, we were always observant as our son grew and changed. Within the year, the nighttime walking ceased as abruptly as it began.

As a toddler, Mark loved gazing at clouds, finding meaning in their shapes. He was carefree, a watcher absorbing his surroundings. Mark was an inquisitive child with early and charming idiosyncrasies. He was, as his father still refers to the young Mark, a "honey of a child." He sensed the emotions of others. He had an unusual ability to discern the intricacies of personality. He knew whom he liked and whom he did not. On one occasion, much to our embarrassment, he told a dinner guest to his face, "I don't like you. I really don't like you." There was silence all around.

Later, I explained that if he ever felt that way again, he should tell me in private because "those words can make someone feel very bad." In that instance, however, Mark was on target; we later discovered that the man he did not like was someone who, indeed, could not be trusted. Even today, as an adult, I have confidence in Mark's measure of a man or woman. He was not wrong then, and he is seldom wrong now.

As Houston and I settled into Philadelphia, we found what we hoped would be the ideal prekindergarten for Mark; it was a version of today's charter school. It was a liberal 1970s project, boasting in its brochure a comfortable mixture of white and black children from various neighborhoods in Philadelphia. It was located in the university neighborhood near Houston's new workplace, so delivering Mark to school in the mornings would be easy. The profile of the preschool fit our idea of the perfect place for our son to continue his early learning.

We soon realized, however, that most of the black children in the center were scholarship kids, sponsored by city organizations. Most of the white children lived near the University of Pennsylvania in a middle-class area and were not on scholarship. On one particular afternoon, as I helped Mark pack up his belongings, his teacher, who was African American, casually informed me that Mark was the only black child in the preschool class whose parents were professionally employed. I wondered about the intent of her utterance. Days later, in an uncomfortable parent-teacher conference, she informed me that Mark was a "disturbance to the learning environment. He is too talkative. He answers too many of my questions. He doesn't give others a chance," she explained in her overly articulated English.

In her opinion, Mark had been privileged in his learning, and he set the bar too high for the classroom. Her solution was to have Mark sit quietly in the corner, and he did so repeatedly, a signal to the other children that he had misbehaved. I was furious at her silencing of our son. I started dropping in unannounced to see how Mark was being treated. During one such visit, I witnessed three of his classmates marching the stairs to a childish chant, "Mark is a bad boy. Mark is a bad boy." They pointed at him and giggled. Neither the children nor the teacher knew I was watching. Perhaps this teacher felt we were "slumming" by enrolling our black child in the center. In fact, we were trying to find a place of comfort for Mark where he would learn about both worlds in which he lived.

Soon after, out of the blue, Mark came home begging for a haircut. "But you don't need a haircut," I chimed. "Your hair is easy for you to brush just the way it is." Mark's hair formed a circle of soft curls about his face. I asked the teacher at school about his repeated request for us to cut his hair. His teacher, of a darker complexion than either Mark or me, and with hot-combed and tightly styled hair, told me that the other boys (meaning the other black boys) had clearly defined parts in their hair, and Mark did not. The teacher thought that Mark's hair did not fit in with the styles of the other boys, and she had somehow persuaded Mark that it was wrong to wear his hair curly and long. Now he wanted to be like the other children. I was dumbstruck by the teacher's rigidity. I had no answer for this woman in whose care I had placed our son.

At that moment, I resolved to find another place for Mark. This proved difficult. In other prekindergarten classrooms we tried, teachers suggested Mark would be even more ostracized entering a school group late, and, furthermore, Mark did not want to leave his new friends at the center. Unhappily, we kept our son where he was, and we took him to a black barber for a very short haircut. Every morning, he and I brushed his hair, trying to create a decisive part. Mark, as it turned out, had not matched the liberal school's profile of a black kid from the surrounding, low-income neighborhood. He was, seemingly, too different even for a preschool that claimed to enroll a mixture of racial groups.

The following year, Houston and I visited a number of independent schools in Philadelphia and finally chose to register Mark as a kindergartner at Germantown Friends School (GFS), a primary and secondary school with impressive academic requirements and a history of fair treatment toward children of color. When we visited, we loved seeing the children display their independence and enjoy taking part in their own day-to-day decision making. We saw one little boy, about seven or eight years old, wandering around with a violin strapped across his shoulder. We asked if he was lost, and he responded, "Oh no, I just stopped to see my kindergarten teacher. I'm on my way to my violin lesson." Houston and I appreciated that the school chose to maintain its campus in the Germantown section of Philadelphia amidst a large, long-standing African American population. Learning to read, to share, and to play were the only goals of the kindergarten year at GFS, and Mark accomplished these happily. The highlight of his kindergarten year was his teacher, Mrs. Workman, who seemed to cast magic for all of her students. Mark's second African American teacher in just a few years, she was a striking and positive contrast to his preschool teacher. Mrs. Workman was calm and respectful toward Mark and all his classmates. Their opinions and preferences mattered to her.

By his third-grade year, Mark and I began having regular afternoon talks about his classes at school. I was no longer exclusively a stay-at-home mom, but I could carve out time in the middle of the day because I was a graduate student with some flexibility. Mark and I stretched out on the living-room rug, and he regaled me with stories about the kid whose "frog had the hiccups" or his teacher, who shook his hand at the end of every day. "She shook my hand, *and* she patted me on the back," he said once. "All because I had a good spelling test." He was delighted at the special attention. During these after-school moments, Mark and I added friendship to our mother-son relationship.

One day during one of our check-ins, I asked, "So, how was school today?"

Broadly smiling with third-grade confidence, Mark replied, "I tried out for the school talent show today."

Curious, since I had not known of a talent show, I wondered what performance our son gave. "So what did you do, sweetheart?" I asked, thinking he had recited a poem or sung a school song.

"I played the piano," he jauntily replied, chomping on a peanut butter sandwich. Puzzled by his nonchalance, I inquired further; Mark had never taken formal lessons for the piano. He explained, "You know. I played the piece *you* taught me." I blushed to think what I had actually taught him: "Chopsticks." He had become quite good at it. Surely, however, his rendition of "Chopsticks" was not suitable competition for his schoolmates at Germantown Friends. But Mark was afforded his fifteen minutes of fame. The next evening, he told us he had not made the second cut at tryouts; he would not be on the final program. "But that's OK," he said. "I'll try next year. Everybody couldn't make it." Many years later, this was the confident Mark I remembered during the long nights when I cried and wished for his wellness.

adolescence

HOUSTON AND I HAD ALWAYS planned for Mark to spend some years in public school so that he would experience differences of race and privilege not always found in a private school setting. For Mark's middle school, we chose a public school nearby. Both Houston and I had attended public schools during childhood; we believed Mark would benefit as well. We felt confident that we had given our son a good start at Germantown Friends for his early years. We discussed with Mark the change from private to public, and after a few days of deliberation, he accepted our proposal. He already had several friends at neighborhood schools. His transition happened easily. Mark excelled in his academic subjects and earned a spot on the Junior Honor Roll his first year at Plymouth Whitemarsh Middle School. The following year, we bought a home a few blocks away, and Mark had to change schools. At Wissahickon Middle School, he trained hard at track and became what his friends called a "track star." He won medals in the 70-meter dash and the 800-meter relay. Popularity was a new experience. He seemed happy.

About this same time, the telephone became Mark's bodily extension. Track friends called, and together they spent inordinate amounts of time deciding small details, such as which runner "absolutely, positively needed to pass the baton smoothly in the next relay." Girl-calls, with Mark saying very little, became a ritual of the evening, with an appreciative increase on weekends. Preadolescence had arrived. Our long after-school talks in the living room became a thing of the past; I discovered I had been replaced by the continuously ringing telephone. Houston and I gradually became accustomed to making numerous trips to the mall, especially on

Saturday evenings, and waiting for the final pick-up request at 11:00 PM, as close to mall closing as possible. When Mark later became ill with bipolar disorder, I wished for those mellow Saturday evenings of driving carpool. I wished for a son whose only transgressions were overusing the telephone or staying out beyond the curfew hour. I would have given anything to hear again the joyous, carefree laughter of Mark's middle school years.

In his early teenage years, Mark still enjoyed shopping expeditions with me. I remember one day in particular. We entered the mall in late afternoon sunshine. Night had descended without my realizing it as we were walking mall corridors, window shopping, and talking. As I passed one of the entrances, the darkness surprised me. Exhausted and hungry, we caught the scent of grilled hot dogs, onions, and fries. Both hot dog lovers, we knew *this* was dinner. We found a nearby table and people-watched as we ate. Between bites, Mark told me anecdotes about his track meets and how the team's hard training each day after school paid off in wins. He plied me with details of who was dating whom in his class. We talked so easily with each other.

As Mark approached ninth grade, Houston and I talked with him again about where he would attend school, this time for his final four years before college. We proposed that he re-enter Germantown Friends, where I had been hired the previous year to teach high school English. I had just completed my PhD in linguistics at Temple University and, at the suggestion of a GFS faculty friend, had applied to fill an unexpected vacancy in the English department's upper school. One of the additional benefits of teaching at GFS was that my son could attend the school tuition-free, provided he passed all the entrance exams. It seemed like a perfect situation.

When we made the proposal to Mark about returning to GFS, he looked at us as if we had suggested a military academy.

"But, Mark, your friends are there waiting for you. You'll have a great time," I explained.

Mark's face was incredulous. "These *are* my friends, Mom," he said, referring to his track buddies and all of the friends he had made during the past three years at public school. "I want to stay with them."

In the face of his resistance, I put an idea on the table for him to consider: "If you go back to GFS, Mark, we can make a deal. Stay one year, and if you don't like it, you can enroll in the local high school."

We wanted Mark to be content with school, but we also wanted him to give GFS another chance. We knew if he still wanted to go to college, GFS was the best place for him to be during high school. Mark reconsidered the proposition and applied to go back to Germantown Friends. After completing ninth grade, with old friendships re-established and no pressure from me, he made his own choice to finish high school at GFS.

In his new school setting, Mark discovered a love for European history. Prior to this time, learning history had consisted of memorizing a rush of indistinguishable dates. But his ninth-grade teacher described historical happenings in great detail, with a flair that mesmerized his young students. "It's like it just happened," Mark exclaimed. "And he's really a great guy! He says I have a good mind for history." So when Mark brought home a grade of C in history, we were puzzled and definitely not pleased. In answer to our questioning ("But why?"), he responded, "Anybody can get an A if they study. I love the stuff. I *know* it. I have a good mind for it; Mr. K. said so!" Mark could recite details of battles and their dates and rehearse the occurrences leading up to military conflicts, but he was nonchalant about turning in his homework.

His history teacher patiently explained, "Mark, what final grade can I possibly give you if you don't turn in daily assignments?"

Mark finally came to understand that studying and completing homework were necessary parts of enjoying the battles detailed in the history books. In written grade reports, teachers sometimes reported, "Mark could apply himself more earnestly." He was not working to his potential. By the time he entered his junior year at GFS, Mark's study habits had improved greatly, and his grades followed.

Throughout his four years of high school, Mark's popularity never waned. One weekend, he had four engagements in his planner: three parties and a basketball game. We told him he could choose two; studying at home was a necessary event. "You don't have to stay out every weekend. We have great space here for a party," we reminded him. He never took us up on our offer.

Sometime after his GFS graduation, Mark finally told us why he had never invited classmates home for a party. "You know why I never wanted to give a party at our house?" he began. "I would not have been able to keep people from drinking alcohol and smoking grass, and you would have freaked."

I was surprised by his unsolicited revelation. Even though Houston and I had grown up on the fringes of the 1960s, we had not been drug users or experimenters. We taught Mark not to use drugs, and when it came to our son, we wore blinders. Mark told us that he and his track friends never used drugs or drank. They called themselves the "milk brigade," Mark said, because milk was all they ever drank when they were in training. We later discovered, however, that Mark smoked marijuana and drank alcohol with other friends during that period. As I think back, I recognize that there were gaping holes in Mark's narrative that I failed to see at the time.

Years afterward, when I forced myself to replay our conversations, it became clear that Mark had offered us a carefully edited version of his high school exploits, and I had completely fallen for it. Houston and I had both believed his claims of abstinence. Today, however, we pinch ourselves, wondering how we could ever have been so naïve. I cannot help but think that by dabbling with grass in those early years, Mark had started down a path that would ultimately lead to his use of marijuana and cocaine as self-medication for his bipolar disorder.

During his junior and senior years of high school, Mark began to have noticeable bouts of anger. He became unusually grumpy. The least little misstep was a major stumble; he ran out of glue one night for a science project, and suddenly the entire project "wasn't that good anyway." We always reasoned these moments away. One of his particularly intense rages occurred during the winter of his junior year.

One evening after dinner, he casually informed us that a few classmates were going to Vermont to ski. "I'm going with them," he announced. He sounded so sure that I remember turning around to look at him when he said it, to see if he was joking. In fact, he asserted that he was going to drive our Jeep, which, purely for convenience, Houston and I had loaned him for his last two years of high school.

"Whatever gave you the notion that we would allow you to drive our car that distance with friends?" I asked, incredulous. Mark had assumed, without asking, that we would provide his room, board, and ski vacation expenses, and that he could drive our family car. This was not the first time we had faced such a clash of values, and it was for us one of the drawbacks of placing Mark in a private school among so many children of privilege.

Mark argued and pleaded passionately, "But I told them I would drive!" His pride was at stake. He was furious with our decision, but he said nothing more.

I asked again, still curious, "How could you assume that we would give permission for that?" Houston and I were in complete agreement; five teenaged boys on the road to Vermont without supervision was not our idea of common sense.

A week later, when I asked Mark to wash the dishes before he went out, his temper went into overdrive. With no overture, he began to shout profanities. He told us what he was and was not going to do. He yelled at his father, "And you said you *allowed* me to use the Jeep. That is my car. You gave it to me, you bastard! Now you're taking it away." His ranting escalated into more name-calling. Mark claimed we treated him as if he were in prison. He accused us of treating him like a kid and shouted that we never allowed him to be like the other guys.

"That trip to Vermont was nothing. You were just afraid we'd trash your precious car," he said with a smirk.

I began to plead for calm, "Come on, let's talk, Mark. What's really bothering you?"

"What do you know about anything?" he shouted back at me.

At the rude, harsh tone of his voice, Houston turned abruptly and commanded, "You will not talk that way in this house. Get it together or get out." Mark knew we did not tolerate insolence in our home. Furthermore, Houston despised Mark's use of disrespectful language, especially toward me.

Mark stormed into the city that rainy night, on foot with no coat. He slammed the door so hard the sound reverberated throughout the house. He left his whereabouts unknown long enough to make us uneasy. Two hours later, he called from a phone booth a couple of miles away and sheepishly said, "Dad, I'm really sorry. Will you come get me? I'm soaked."

The next day, Mark apologized to us both. Mark always apologized. The previous evening had been a shock to us. We did not talk with Mark about what had happened. Once his sudden rages passed, we forgot them, like flash storms. Within a day or so, Mark returned to his balanced, amiable self, almost as if the incident had never happened.

In the privacy of our bedroom, Houston and I talked about Mark's rage. We rationalized that the violently harsh moments were due to what I called, "hypersized adolescent moments and hormones in overdrive." We never gave the outbursts any more credence. In retrospect, I wonder whether what we witnessed in those early days was much more than the result of turbulent adolescence. If we had investigated Mark's explosive mood swings or asked for medical advice, would we have considered the possibility that our son was suffering the symptoms of a psychological disorder? At that time, I did not know the term *bipolar disorder*. I knew almost nothing about mental illness. But my world soon would change.

university life

MARK WANTED TO ATTEND COLLEGE on the East Coast. After visiting several universities with his father, he decided on the University of Pennsylvania. We were curious about his choice of school since he had lived in Philadelphia most of his life. His response was thoughtful: "I know Philadelphia, and I like it. I won't have to learn my way around a new city. I can concentrate on campus and what's there." Much later, we could not help but wonder if Mark, even then, knew he might need to be close to home and family. By early spring, he had been accepted into Penn for the following fall. I stopped preparing for a mother-son separation. If I needed to see him, he was only a phone call away. A calm descended for all of us. We focused on the rituals of high school graduation.

Graduation from Germantown Friends involved a flurry of activity, with picture taking at every final venture: the last time with his track friends at a meet, his last time on stage at GFS, his last time with his best girl friend, the last time with a particular teacher. Mark's grandparents, our nieces and nephews, Mark's aunts and uncles, and our long-standing family friends arrived in Philadelphia to celebrate Mark's graduation. Mark was the center. Occasionally, I look back at the numerous photo albums from that single, frozen moment. The number of pictures makes it seem like a year's worth of festivities. It stuns me to realize that half the people celebrating that day still have no idea that Mark is ill.

Once we delivered him to his university home at Penn, a matter of a few miles, Mark attempted to settle into dormitory life. Houston and I decided not to bother him with frequent telephone calls. We tried to give him breathing space and a sense of freedom. We set no obligations about visits home. Mark called after two weeks, leaving the message, "Haven't heard from you. What's happening back there?" His call was a surprise. I certainly had not detached, but I had expected Mark to relish his freedom and disconnection from home and parents. We returned his call immediately, and Houston arranged to meet him for lunch. The following month, I called and set up a lunchtime meeting between his classes and mine. I was now at Penn, too. I had left Germantown Friends for an administrative and teaching position at the University of Pennsylvania the year Mark graduated high school. From time to time, I would bump into one of my former students from GFS on campus. I thought I would see Mark in the same random fashion, but we seldom met by chance. Penn was a large campus; it seemed to absorb our separate lives.

During our scheduled lunch, as I chatted on about my classes and people I had met, I realized Mark was unusually quiet. He was reticent, meditative, and, actually, uninteresting. He had nothing to talk about. This was certainly not normal for Mark. He was typically full of life, with an ironic sense of humor and the latest reports from the R&B and hip-hop music world. I could always count on a good laugh when I was with Mark. That day, his conversation was nil and his face expressionless. Once in a while, a forced smile broke through. I consoled myself thinking he probably had not found his campus niche yet. Maybe he was even a bit homesick. I made conversation about extracurricular activities, clubs, and volunteer groups he could join. I probably sounded like a sappy summer-camp counselor. When I asked about his roommate, Mark sighed and said matter-of-factly, "He doesn't like my music. He goes to bed early, and I need music to do my homework." He and his roommate eventually came to an accord about their differences in lifestyle and set a schedule for work, but he and Raoul never carved out a friendship.

As we parted that day, I felt the chill of distance. Mark's hug had no heart. He assured me he was fine, so I had nothing to hang my distress on. When I turned back to the table for my books, I saw that most of Mark's sandwich was untouched.

I realize now that Mark was probably depressed. At the time, I had no idea what depression looked like. Houston and I still knew nothing of bipolar disorder or its signs. All my life I had misunderstood depression as a sign of weakness, a lapse in fortitude when circumstances were difficult to manage. People in my family did not admit to feeling depressed. My parents urged me always to "keep moving" at all costs, and "complete what is expected," euphemisms they never clearly explained. They simply assumed that I would never succumb to any weakness. Unknowingly, I thought the same was true for our son. He would just keep moving. I later asked Mark about that particular lunch. He remembered feeling my discomfort and admitted to having a sense of aloofness. "I can't really explain it. You were there, but it was hard to connect. I was just not feeling quite right, kind of empty," he said. In his writing, Mark tries to express the barrenness:

I feel empty
less than nothing
like a laughing stock
a clown
melancholy and manic
hopeless and terrified
a semblance of my true self
hallucinations haunt me
racing thoughts mock me
driving me into a fog of insanity
thick white clouds
obscure my vision
I no longer have dreams

my aspirations are none
I throw a white towel
to the canvas of life.

Mark's junior year at Penn was highlighted by the appearance of a girlfriend who Mark said "understands me. She's not superficial like the others. She knows what life is about." Mark had met Shelly at the same shopping mall he had frequented as a young man in high school. She was not from the university; she worked retail in the mall and was thinking of returning to school. Mark began to talk incessantly about Shelly, his new girlfriend. We thought he had been dating someone else seriously for the past few months. Mark's habit of shifting from one sweetheart to the next began shortly after he entered college. Was my sensitive son becoming something of a cad? Trying not to be the meddling mother, I nodded, smiled, and pretended to accept it.

The summer before his senior year, Mark decided to move off campus and live with Shelly for his final year at Penn. Ever so quickly, they seemed to lock into plans for the future. They shared the rent, and we helped. We were never party to Mark's behavior during that time, but Shelly later told me that Mark experienced stormy mood shifts during his final year. Sometimes he drank excessively. They kept this secret. Shelly was in love. Mark thought he was.

In 1992, his senior year, Mark had taken on heavy responsibilities at Penn. He decided to reactivate a defunct drama/arts initiative for African American students. In previous years, the African American Arts Alliance had dissolved due to lack of funding and campus enthusiasm. With a university permit in hand, Mark committed himself and like-minded friends to breathe life back into this arts program by staging August Wilson's play *Fences*. He asked for my volunteer help coaching the actors; I obliged. During the ten months of pre- and post-production, I marveled at Mark's abounding exuberance. He solicited funds and helped orchestrate bake sales. I witnessed his flights of intense anger at crew members who were dragging their feet on the job, and his high fives when people knew their lines. I observed Mark contemplative, in huddles with the crew, making production decisions. I supported him with extra cash when the group needed to eat. Houston gave dollars when a prop was needed for the play. I saw Mark darting about like Peter Pan, lovingly supportive, especially of the young women on board. Everyone involved in *Fences* seemed to understand and respect Mark. He became central to his on-campus circle of drama friends. The play opened to standing-room-only audiences. As Mark rehearsed into the night, night after night, he seemed to forget Shelly was waiting for him at their apartment. I offered no comment.

Years later, I revisited Mark's directing of *Fences* during those final months at Penn. I never knew what to call the wildness I saw. Now I understand his unpredictability, his episodic instability. What I saw then was the slightly eccentric artist at work. Shelly was ever-faithful. She had been the glue that kept him together.

On closing night, after the final performance of *Fences*, the actors and crew broke set and carried their festivities into the morning hours. Houston and I offered our congratulatory messages early on. The newly formed drama group had been enormously successful. We felt proud of what we had helped to nurture. The evening seemed calm and appropriately celebratory. Shelly came to the final performance, bearing champagne. She did not stay for the party. It was obvious from their cryptic, chilly exchange that she and Mark were in conflict.

Two weeks later, Mark marched at graduation and officially left the University of Pennsylvania. During his four years at Penn, Mark's grades were well above average, and he now entertained thoughts of graduate school. Within a couple of months after graduation, with no public explanation, Mark and Shelly went their separate ways.

life shifts

MARK HAD NOT THOUGHT OF film study for graduate school until he discussed the possibility with Jon, his best friend from high school. Jon was already a student at Tisch School of the Arts at New York University. He convinced Mark to apply for a space in the film production program.

Mark's application was down to the wire. He liked the headiness of working under pressure. He never complained about running out of time. He excitedly set his mind to completing the required five-minute, self-made video to accompany his Tisch application and believed nothing could go wrong. He persuaded a friend at the radio station at Penn to lend him camera equipment for one day. Now he only needed an idea for the film that would be part of his application package.

While at Penn, Mark had worked with twelve-year-old Steven as part of Penn's community-school mentoring program. Mark knew he wanted Steven to be a part of the film even before he chose his film topic. For close to a year, the two of them had been working on math and writing skills. They had recently talked about Mark's desire to go to film school. Now, Steven was happy to be a part of Mark's project. With permission from home, he spent an entire Saturday with Mark, filming activities that he liked: playing basketball, watching the ferry as it crossed the Delaware River, and riding the subway home. Mark set the continuous day's shoot to the music of John Coltrane's "My Favorite Things." The title, topic, and subject were a perfect match, a rendition of a day in the life of a young boy. Mark sent off the short film of the same name as part of his application. When Mark called home the evening after his film shoot, he was euphorically happy. Everything had progressed as he had wanted. Weeks later, he received notice of his acceptance to Tisch for the fall of 1993. The faculty thought his film was innovative and offered him a small stipend.

Mark loved everything about New York, Tisch, and filmmaking. At Penn, he had always been in search of an anchor; in New York, he felt totally at home. Mark and Jon harmoniously shared a New York apartment. At Mark's invitation, Houston and I visited Greenwich Village whenever we could. We enjoyed people watching and eating out with our son. It was delicious to be in his company. Several times, I went to New York alone. Mark and I walked for blocks and blocks in Manhattan, laughing, talking, and peering into department store windows, pretending to buy what we saw.

Houston and I were gratified that Mark enjoyed classes at Tisch and his living arrangements in New York. He called us often in Philadelphia from his sixth-story Village apartment. When he did, I heard the delight in his voice mingled with the din of Manhattan traffic. Houston and I committed ourselves to helping Mark financially as much as we could. The late 1980s and early 1990s were the heyday of black independent filmmaking in the United States, and Mark wanted to be a part of that surge. During his year at Tisch, his passion for film pushed him into overdrive. He worked through the night to complete deadlines. Sometimes, one night blended into the next. When he was not working, he went to parties. Sleep was not on his schedule.

Mark's requests for additional money that year seemed odd to us since we were already sending him a regular stipend each month. But his explanations were always reasonable and persuasive: "Mom, I need just two hundred dollars more to pay the editor to finish my film. I had more footage than I thought." About two weeks later, he asked his father for a few dollars to get groceries for the coming week: "I overspent on my film, Dad. I didn't know I had to pay so much for the sound of a buzzing lamppost!" Houston sent the extra money. With each phone call, there seemed to be new necessities. We knew film production was expensive and that Mark was competing with a number of older, self-supporting student filmmakers. Still, money seemed to slip through his fingers. At home in Philadelphia, Houston and I were extremely busy with our own work. We were not always attentive to the details and implications of Mark's money demands. During the Tisch year, Houston and I believed Mark's requests for necessities. We fell for what we later learned were his small deceptions. At the time, we had no reason to suspect his explanations. Flanked by phone calls coming in and payments going out, we had yet to realize what was truly happening to our son.

Mark finished his first year. He invited us to the public screening of his and his classmates' original eight-minute color films, followed by faculty reviews. Excitedly, we sat with hands clenched as Mark introduced his own project, *Ain't No Love*. The film's black protagonist, Andre, in spite of his girlfriend's urging, is not interested in completing a GED. All he cares about is selling drugs and living a life of crime. After he and his best friend are shot during an argument with another drug dealer, and his friend dies, Andre contemplates revenge. His girlfriend demands that he choose between their relationship or a life of crime. Andre chooses the girl. The film ends as the other dealer shoots a policeman and then, later, himself.

I was completely absorbed as I watched Mark's film. I was incredibly proud of his talent. He had successfully backlit the outdoor scenes with only sunlight, a difficult feat that earned him praise from several of his classmates. During the post-film discussion, a few of the faculty at Tisch questioned Mark's use of guns in the film and his focus on violence. Houston and I thought his choice of topic was a thoughtful examination of another segment of black life. We did not think twice about the fact that Mark had been the only student in his class to depict drug dealing, street violence, and suicide in his final film. Years later, the thought of Mark's film gives me chills.

At the end of his first year at Tisch, without another tuition scholarship or funding for more film production, Mark decided to apply to other graduate film schools that focused on film criticism and theory. The program at the University of Southern California (USC) included courses in sociology, history, and the theory of film, and would complement the production courses he had taken at Tisch. Impressed with his work at Tisch and his strong letters of recommendation, the graduate film school at USC awarded Mark a generous stipend with full tuition benefits. The fellowship obligated him to maintain strong grades in his coursework. If he lived modestly, he would be able to study without money worries until he completed his doctoral degree. When we heard the news, Houston and I were walking along a Manhattan thoroughfare, on our way to meet Mark for a New York dinner. My cell phone rang; Mark could not wait to give us the fantastic news. He was deliriously happy.

Mark made arrangements to leave the East Coast for California. At twenty-three, he was looking forward to living on the Left Coast, as he called it. His preparations were focused and purposeful. It was Mark's idea that we all drive to California together. "You'll be able to see where I live, Mom. I know you'll like that. We can visit some of the places we saw on our last cross-country trip together," he explained. Houston and I discussed the possibility of the California trip and realized it could be a bonding experience. The proposed graduate school journey reminded us fondly of our last family trip to California when Mark was six years old. We found no reason not to proceed with his suggestion. With AAA maps and reservations for reasonable lodgings, the three of us set out for Los Angeles in the Toyota that Houston and I leased for

Mark. We visited the Grand Canyon, the Painted Desert, and a few friends along the way.

Just outside Los Angeles, as we approached the end of our placid, ten-day family trip, Mark's temper flared over a very small matter: highway directions. We were moving through small towns on our way into the city. Houston had one set of directions into Los Angeles, and Mark had another. Mark read aloud his directions, and Houston authoritatively contradicted him. Mark started shouting, "You don't know what you're talking about. You always know so much!"

"I've been here before, Mark," Houston said with a fatherly confidence and kept driving.

Mark began to yell louder, as if volume would increase his credibility. Houston's voice rose to match Mark's volume. Mark then began shouting accusatory names and obscene remarks with even more intensity. His booming voice seemed to rock the car and invade my body. I grew afraid of my own son. As Mark continued to rant, Houston realized we were in a precarious situation. He tried in vain to interrupt Mark's now incoherent words by speaking slowly and deliberately. He pulled over to the curb and turned off the ignition. By this time, Mark was completely out of control. He turned his fury on me as I attempted to intervene and offer a possible solution to the problem of directions.

"Who do you think you are? Shut up! You don't know anything!" Mark shouted.

"Just stop it!" Houston yelled, trying to end the incident.

The verbal conflict only escalated, and the space inside the car was suddenly too small for all of us. I opened the door to free myself from the inside commotion that was now threatening to spill onto the streets of the small L.A. suburb. Strangers stared and quickly turned away, trying to pretend everything was normal. I was horribly embarrassed.

Outside the car, I hoped my desertion would help dissolve the argument between Mark and his father. When it did not, I shouted to Mark as furiously as I could, "Get out and follow me. Now!" He made swift eye contact and then followed me. Once out, he continued his tirade one decibel lower. I walked rapidly with him trailing behind. Whatever he said, I nodded in agreement. I thought he would run out of steam or realize that we were walking away from our car in a strange town. Mark had morphed into an irrational being I did not recognize. He accused me of walking away from a legitimate quarrel. He shouted accusations, insisting, for instance, that I had never stood up for him in past arguments with his father. I nervously glanced back at the car and saw Houston standing on the sidewalk beckoning for me to return. I attempted to turn back, but Mark would not let me pass. He continued to berate and criticize, moving in front of me each time I tried to move away. All of a sudden, I realized I did not recognize the man whose lips were moving, whose face was distorted with rage. I froze. Would this person hit me? A new fear hummed through my body. I could not let this man know I was afraid. I could see Houston in the distance; I could not call out to him or begin to run.

As he raged, Mark's crude and nasty accusations brought flashbacks. The word "bitch," spit from my son's mouth, was jolting and confusing. His insults were gritty street words I had heard the night of our home invasion. Those were not Mark's words. In that Los Angeles instant, I was transported back to a Philadelphia evening in 1981.

In September of that year, 1981, two black men broke into our Philadelphia home. Mark was ten, almost eleven. Houston and I were returning home after a vacation with friends in Connecticut.

Mark had been visiting his two sets of grandparents in Washington, DC. On our way back, we stopped in DC to pick him up, and the three of us returned home to Philadelphia a day early to prepare for Mark's first day of school. That same evening, just after the eleven o'clock news, Houston and I heard a loud, dull thud that reverberated throughout the house. It was not one of the normal creaking and settling noises we sometimes heard. We both startled and jumped up at the same time; I headed for Mark's room on the third floor, hoping he had only fallen out of bed. Houston leapt down the stairs to check the first floor. We knew the burglar alarm was set for the night; we turned it on each evening, like clockwork, before climbing the stairs. On the first floor, Houston encountered a stranger, an armed man who had forcibly entered our hallway through the basement door. The calm of that night was forever shattered when I heard Houston call to me, "There is someone in the house. Stay where you are."

After kicking and punching Houston to the floor, the intruder pointed a gun at Houston's head and forced me down the stairs to turn off the alarm and open the front door. "Get down here or I'll put a bullet in his head," he threatened. My teeth clattered with fear, and I was baffled. Did he want to get out? Once I had turned off the alarm and turned the key in the lock, a second man pushed his way into our home. The two intruders brought weapons, terror, shouts of "bitch," "cunt," "nigger," and threats of death. That evening on the first floor, I was raped many times at the point of a knife and a gun while my husband and son remained helpless, gagged and bound upstairs on our king-sized bed. We barely escaped with our lives.

Throughout the evening, Mark was oddly calm. Once the two men had gone and the house had grown silent, Mark was the one who negotiated his way through the darkened house to find a knife in the kitchen to cut the rope around his father's hands and feet.

Mark had been tied with wrapping yarn and was able to free himself. Houston was tied with rope, and I had been hog-tied with stereo wire. Mark was the hero of the night, but he said very little after the event.

I wrote about this ordeal of the soul twelve years later in a memoir, *Surviving the Silence*, a book Mark told me he supported in the writing. Years after the publication of the book, Mark confessed he had never read any part of it. In his poetry, however, he tried to capture his sorrow:

> *Mom,*
> *When they tried*
> *to steal you away from me,*
> *they violated your body,*
> *but could not capture your mind.*
> *It still held love for me*
> *even when you could not*
> *bring yourself to hold me.*
> *You pushed me away with your hands,*
> *but adored me with your eyes.*

During our upsetting quarrel on the streets approaching Los Angeles, Mark's booming adult male voice brought back to me the hateful, sordid threats of that night in 1981. Silently, I pleaded for my life once again; the present and past were colliding. In my fog, I began to hurry toward the car and my husband, as if I could outrun the haunting, vivid memories. Mark was still behind me. I could hear his breathing. I began to calm down as Houston came into view.

As we neared the car, Mark seemed to snap out of it, as if he were also returning to the present. His speech slowed, and his breathing became more normal. He became aware that he had been acting strangely. As we walked, we fell into the same cadence, and Mark spoke with less intensity. I was so overwhelmed and traumatized that

I repeated nothing to Houston. Since Mark and I were both quiet by the time we arrived at the car, Houston assumed I had talked Mark back to reason during our walk. We got in the car, checked directions, and proceeded to L.A. There was tension in the air, but Mark apologized for his anger and behavior. Houston and I, in turn, expressed regrets for any misunderstanding. One of us quipped about the pressures of driving such a long distance, cooped up in a car packed to the hilt. The strained stillness took us into the city.

Mark was horrified when I told him recently of my memory of that Los Angeles encounter. He has not stopped asking my forgiveness.

another home

AFTER SETTLING INTO OUR HOTEL for the night, Houston and I awoke the following morning to Mark's apologies. There were no further rages, no misunderstandings, but we remained careful. Days later, Houston and I almost doubted what had happened in the car. It was as if we had all been held captive in a bad dream. I now believe that Mark was feeling the side effects of drug and alcohol withdrawal. We had been on the road together for almost ten days.

After breakfast the first day in L.A., Mark showed us his new living space in what realtors called the mid-Wilshire district. Living here was an advantage because Mark would be near the university. When I looked closely at Mark's new space, I noticed razor wire high up on the fencing surrounding the brightly pink, beautifully maintained complex. It became clear that Mark was living in a marginal area; we later learned that the adjacent section of the city was then called South Central, where, allegedly, drugs were available on every corner. In Los Angeles, it is difficult to distinguish between the poor and the posh. The lawns are all the same—always green, always impeccable, and always alluring. But Mark was definitely living in a rough area.

Houston and I headed back to Philadelphia, leaving Mark with his share of unopened boxes, an unmade bed, and promises of "See you at Christmas!" Mark was sad to see us leave but still jauntily confident as he dropped us off at Los Angeles International Airport. I waved, sighed, and fought back tears. I prayed he would perform well at the university. At that time, I had no idea our son was regularly using marijuana and that we were leaving him in a garden of temptation.

From August to December 1994, we stayed in very close touch by telephone. Mark gave us regular updates on his new L.A. life. After a few months, we began to hear a baby's cry in the background, and Mark, on occasion, asked if I wanted to speak with Lisa, someone I had never met. I usually agreed since I was not at all sure how I was supposed to react. Mark's telephone affect was vague. When I asked Mark if he had more than a friendship with Lisa, he responded, "Not really." When I asked if she was a classmate, he said, "Not really, but she's thinking of going back to school." He was consistently evasive. When Houston or I called, Lisa always seemed to be there. Mark insisted, "She's only staying for a few nights." When I asked if she was coming with him to Philadelphia for Christmas, he said, "No, she has to work." Two months later, Mark invited Lisa and her two-year-old daughter to share his apartment, creating an instant family. Everything happened so quickly that I wondered if Mark had met Lisa on the very day of our flight back home to Philly. He told us he first saw her at an L.A. stoplight. Initially, his version of the encounter sounded romantic. Later, I wondered if he had stopped at the light to purchase drugs.

Christmas finally arrived, and Mark came home as promised. He was alone and in good spirits. I vividly remember our cheery greetings at the front door of our Philadelphia home and Houston's and Mark's bear hugs. As soon as Mark and I made eye contact, I caught his enigmatic half smile. I sensed he had something to reveal. We moved into the living room and began small talk about gifts, how good he looked, and what we were having for Christmas dinner. I had been cooking for several days and dressing the house for the holidays. Houston had reshaped the living room to accommodate a rather large holiday tree. Within our first hour together, Mark informed us that he and Lisa had decided to marry after the new year. He was smiling, and his voice was light and carefree.

Although I had been expecting a surprise, this revelation disturbed me. I doubted seriously Mark's ability to provide for a family of three. I doubted his stability, but there was nothing I could say. Before the evening ended, we were speaking long distance to our future daughter-in-law.

uncertainty

WITH EACH PHONE CALL TO Philadelphia after the Christmas visit, Mark began asking for money. His requests sounded reasonable, usually addressing his need to fix furniture or home appliances: a chair with one leg broken, a television with no sound, a refrigerator needing a new part. Although the telephone kept us loosely connected, Mark was leading a life we knew very little about. He described his problems always in terms of money, specifically his perpetual lack of it. Since he and Lisa were often broke by the end of the month, I wondered if he could be misspending his stipend. Was he trying to support a family on a university fellowship?

Houston and I calmed our misgivings by remembering that, although Mark was young and had made his share of missteps, he had also made a serious commitment to graduate school and had earned a doctoral fellowship. We were proud of him. As parents, we had a fleeting sense that something was off kilter, but we had no label for it. We tried to pull back and allow Mark space to make his new life work. The possibility that he was suffering from a mental disorder did not occur to us.

As time passed, the details of Mark's stories began to grow confusing. In one conversation, he was excited to be working on a major film project with fellow students and a graduate faculty advisor. In another, he was having great difficulty with that same advisor who was giving him assignments he could not understand. In the midst of it all, *Rolling Stone* was supposedly interviewing Mark about a proposed film project. According to Mark, he was continuously away from the apartment due to scheduled film shoots. "I always miss your phone calls," he told me. We began to wonder if

Mark was even doing collaborative film work. We found out later that there was an ongoing film shoot at the school but that Mark's professor had asked him *not* to participate. His attendance was unreliable, and his moods were unpredictable. Mark continued to furnish us with renditions of his L.A. life and to cover his tracks with whatever pretext was handy. Each time I heard his voice, I felt tension, but I could not put my finger on why.

We took no vacation during the summer of 1995. Houston and I felt an inexplicable sense of unease. We decided to rest, read for classes, and visit our ill parents in Washington, DC. By the start of the fall term, one year after leaving Mark in Los Angeles, we became patently aware that Mark's life was not proceeding well. He began to supply us with disastrous stories about his academic department at USC. He claimed his faculty advisor had betrayed him, but he would not give us details. He described his fellow students, who had been his constant companions in previous months, as "shallow hypocrites." Professors were "not teaching accurately." Other students ostracized him. These were Mark's insistent declarations in early September. Accounts of his own behavior were absent. When we questioned him, he became hostile and countered, "You don't believe me?"

Mark's ungrounded descriptions did not match what we knew about the film department at USC. Because of this, we needed more information to clarify what was happening. Houston made a few phone calls to colleagues at USC to try to uncover the facts. Could the department really be falling apart? We discovered, to the contrary, that Mark's reports were mere fantasies and cover-ups for his own rudeness, lapses in attendance, and irresponsibility. Apparently, Mark had also told bewildered classmates stories about his "poor family at home with no money."

Hearing these reports from professors and students both angered and embarrassed me. "He is just acting crazy," I remember saying aloud to Houston. I never thought he might be using drugs.

Mark continued his phone calls to Philadelphia, usually sharing a laundry list of difficulties. Often, he asked for a loan "to help my family." We kept sending him checks. In spite of our generosity, Mark seemed continually dissatisfied with one or both of us, and he did not hesitate to tell us so. It was always a toss-up, who was "it," Houston or me. Mark began to berate us for having a bank account, jobs we enjoyed, and a house of our own, while he "had nothing." We never fought back. Most of the time, I steeled myself for the imminent tirade when Mark called. Somehow, I knew that a wrong word could produce an escalating conflict. After gratifying his every request for money, we grew weary. We began to feel as if we were giving handouts. We hated the ring of the telephone.

Then, out of the blue, as if there had been no tension between Philadelphia and Los Angeles, Mark called to invite us to his master of arts graduation ceremony at USC. We accepted with delight. To be on Mark's good side was heartening. We flew to Los Angeles in May 1996 to see our twenty-five-year-old son graduate once again and to meet his fiancée and her daughter. Houston and I agreed to hide our feelings of anxiety and disappointment until there was a suitable moment alone for a family discussion with Mark. That moment never came.

During the commencement ceremony, Houston and I applauded proudly with the other parents as graduates crossed the stage to receive their degrees. When I saw Mark in his cap and gown, I was suddenly struck by his wraithlike appearance. He looked worn. I began to cry as I applauded even more loudly. Houston, in his excitement, ran up to meet Mark as he descended the stage. Families congregated after the ceremony and moved noisily toward the reception announced in the program. Mark made no mention of our joining his classmates in the postgraduation festivities. He said he had planned "family time with Lisa and her daughter." We were not introduced to any of his teachers. A lone instructor waved in passing. Mark gave a jaunty wave back. We posed for a few pictures and then found ourselves back in the car. Thinking Mark and Lisa had perhaps planned a picnic at Redondo Beach, one of their favorite spots, we got comfortable for what we were told would be a long ride.

When we got to the beach, we walked the boardwalk without conversation. We even passed up having ice cream. Lisa and Mark seemed absorbed in their own world. They walked ahead of us, holding hands. Lisa's daughter, Angela, ran back and forth between them and us, making her own fun. In fact, Mark and Lisa barely spoke to us, and the outing itself became stranger and stranger as the afternoon progressed. We were passing time in a way that prevented talk or any kind of connection.

The next day, on our flight back to Philadelphia, Houston and I were quiet. I remember thinking, What just happened? I felt an emptiness I could not explain. Lisa had been pleasant to us but had made little eye contact during our previous afternoon together, and she spoke almost exclusively to Mark. Her daughter was a lovely, polite two-year-old who called us Grandma and Granddad, as if she had been trained to do so. Reflecting on our day together, I was bewildered. Houston and I retreated into academic work and graded papers all the way home. We had nothing to talk about.

Once we were home, Mark's calls grew infrequent. Into the second week, I tried calling L.A. to check in. There was no answer and no answering machine. The following week, Houston attempted a call, only to hear an automated phone company message: "This is no longer a working number." Both concerned, we confessed to each other how many times we had actually called L.A. without connecting with anyone. In two weeks, we had each called three times. Coupled with the uneasiness we brought back from California, my own anxiety was high. Waiting was all we could do. Four weeks after we returned, Mark called. We sighed with relief. He and Lisa had moved into a different apartment complex. He said, "I forgot to call and give you the number."

Mark and Lisa's phone number shifted another two times within the next two months. We learned later that they changed addresses frequently, trying to outrun bill collectors and overdue rent. During one of his brief phone calls, Mark inadvertently confessed that he had not actually graduated in May with a master's degree, as we had believed. I was furious.

"Why in the world did we travel to L.A. and spend all that time and money for nothing?" I screeched into the phone. "You told us you were getting your master's degree! How could you lie to us?"

His answer was weak: "I thought you would be disappointed if I told you the truth, and it didn't really matter. I was still in the PhD program."

Mark had marched at the May graduation despite the fact that he had not completed all the requirements to earn a master's degree. Since his plan was to complete the PhD program and his work to that point had been exemplary, his department had allowed him to participate in the master's degree ceremony and march with his class. Even with the explanation, I was livid. Mark and I did not talk again for months. He did not call me, and, for once, I did not call him either.

Finally, I broke the dry spell of communication. I never felt comfortable being separated from Mark for long periods. Houston and I were taking some vacation days before the start of classes. I had completed my first book, *Surviving the Silence*, and I called Mark to give him the good news. During my writing process, he had occasionally sent me notes of encouragement, which I always appreciated. When he answered the phone that evening, he seemed to be celebrating as well. There was loud music in the background. The rhythm of his speech was slow and deliberate. He offered me a jovial but crisp, "Congratulations, Mom," yet he seemed detached and distracted, disconnected from my happiness. I felt his distance and uttered a puzzled, "Thanks." The word was barely out of my mouth when I heard Mark hang up the phone. I was confused and bruised by his response.

two

illness made manifest

EXACTLY ONE WEEK LATER, returning home after dinner with friends, we found a voicemail message from my father in Washington, DC.

"Charlotte, where are you? I think Mark is in trouble," he said. "You need to call me."

His voice sounded urgent. I called immediately. My father was not an alarmist; I knew he was worried. Mark had called my father when he could not reach us, and they had talked for almost an hour.

"I couldn't get him to stop talking," my father reported. "When I tried to ask him questions, he didn't seem to understand. I . . . I don't know, honey. He sounded really strange. He wanted to talk to you; he explicitly said, 'I do not want to talk to my father.' You need to call him. Here's the number."

I stopped shivering and calmed myself enough to dial. Houston sat nearby for support. Could Mark be in trouble? We had no idea what it all meant.

When Mark answered at the unfamiliar phone number, I asked immediately, "Mark, where are you? Why are you using this strange number?"

"It's a phone booth in Westwood Village," he told me.

I knew the area well since UCLA is in Westwood. "You're not near home at all. What's going on out there?" I prodded, trying to keep my voice steady.

When he answered instantly, "I don't know, Mom," I thought perhaps he had been in an automobile accident and someone was badly hurt. Perhaps the accident was his fault, and he was upset and confused. Mark continued, "They're watching me, Mom. I can't see them, but I know they're watching me. I don't know what to do. What should I do? Help me, Mom."

I was mystified and stunned into silence. I dared to ask, "Who's watching you, Mark?"

He simply repeated, "I *know* they're watching, Mom. Help me. I don't know what to do."

I heard his panic. It leapt the miles between us. The tone of his voice frightened me. I slid to the floor still holding the telephone. It was my lifeline to Mark. He began to gasp for breath, his words rushing one into another. Helplessly, I looked at Houston and wrote, *He's crying!*

I kept repeating slowly, "It's going to be all right. It's OK, Mark. *Sh-sh-sh*. We'll think of something. It's OK. We're here," like a lullaby. I had no idea what to do. If only I could touch him, I thought.

"Mark, why don't you go home? Isn't Lisa at home?" I asked.

My words startled him, and he shouted, "Oh no! I can't go home. It's not safe there. I can't trust her!" I heard the panic again. I decided I had to slow down the conversation.

"Mark, I need to tell your father what's going on. I know he can help us," I tried to explain.

"No, no, no!" he said emphatically. "Don't tell Dad. He doesn't understand these things."

"What things are you talking about, Mark?" I asked, puzzled.

"You know, the extraterrestrials," he said, waiting for my response.

I nearly dropped the telephone. Mark and I had always had fun talking about and debating the issue of life on other planets. We enjoyed television programs that featured people who claimed to have seen flying saucers. Houston would always say to us, jokingly, "I'm out of here. That's your stuff."

I recovered quickly and said, "It's OK, Mark. Your father has changed his mind about those things. It's safe to tell him now. I think you should talk to your Dad."

When Mark became quiet, I knew he had accepted my feeble explanation. Houston spoke to his son. "I'm here with you, Mark," he said. "What do you want me to do?"

Houston and I frantically wrote notes as he talked to Mark. We tried to figure out what action to take and how to give Mark the support he needed. Whatever he was afraid of was real to him. Speeding through my mind were the words, *Is this a nervous breakdown?*

"Mark, do you want me to come get you?" Houston asked.

Mark sighed as he answered, "Yes . . . I want to come home. Please . . . I'm scared."

Our son's life had tripped over itself. It was August 1996. Within hours, Houston was on a flight to Los Angeles.

Armed with his own brand of courage, an extra airline ticket, and a small bag with a change of clothes for our son, Houston rushed to L.A. with promises of love and safety. Houston left Philadelphia with a mask of bravado. He kissed me good-bye, assuring me he would bring Mark home. I knew he was frightened of what he would find.

We gave Mark the name of a university friend and colleague who lived in L.A. We would ask her to meet him in Westwood Village. Houston and I needed help urgently, and Vera Jackson's name came to both of us as someone reliable in a crisis. I assured Mark, "Vera is a safe person; she understands. You don't know her, but she knows all about you. We've talked so much about you over the years. She will keep you safe until your father gets to L.A." Mark responded positively to the word "safe."

When I called Vera in Los Angeles, she was surprised to hear my voice after such a long period without contact. I was not sure I could ask her for the extraordinary favor of watching our son until Houston got to L.A. We were professional colleagues, not friends with a history of growing up together. When I explained Mark's situation and our need, Vera never hesitated. I was touched by her willingness to help us.

"I'm just so glad I didn't go away this weekend," she said. She went on to explain, "I'd thought about going to a conference in Texas, but then, for no good reason, decided not to go. I guess I was supposed to be here."

After asking for Mark's physical description, she agreed to meet him at a Starbucks in Westwood Village and drive him to her home about an hour away. She ended the conversation with, "I'll just keep him comfortable until Houston gets here."

I remained home in Philadelphia. My task was to prepare for Mark's return. He would need a check-up with our family doctor, I guessed. He obviously needed rest and a change of pace. Mark had never been seriously ill growing up. I was sure his condition was a result of overwork and that he would respond to my care at home, a bit of pampering. I prepared his old room for his arrival and bought groceries. Houston called home when he landed in Los Angeles. I paced and waited for the next call telling me my son was OK. Houston did not call again until morning. The drive to Vera's house, in the dark with sketchy directions, had taken him more time than he had expected. Fearing the worst, I slept little.

Houston telephoned me the next day and described the situation. After arriving at Vera's, he knocked and shouted through the door, "It's Houston."

She called to him, "Come on in. The door's open."

Mark was awake, resting quietly in her arms. "She was holding him like a baby," Houston told me. I heard the strain of incredulity still caught in his voice. "Mark looked at me but didn't seem to really see me. He said, 'Hey, Dad,' but it was like he had just seen me the day before. And it really didn't sound like Mark. It was like someone else's voice calling me 'Dad.' It was really weird. Vera whispered hello."

During the hours it had taken Houston to fly from Philadelphia to Los Angeles and then drive the hour and a half to Vera's home,

Mark had slowly deteriorated. He had been talking nonsense, and Vera had been agreeing with everything he said. Mark had shouted at the top of his lungs off and on during the night, so Vera had asked a male friend to come sit with her "just in case something happened that I couldn't handle." She had watched Mark's moods change over the hours.

"Once my friend arrived, Mark seemed to calm more easily," she explained. Vera told us later that she had been so relieved to see Houston arrive with the morning light.

Within a half hour of Houston's arrival, Mark became extremely agitated. He began to scream obscenities directed only at his father. His volume increased, and neighbors began to peer from their doorways. Houston told me Mark frightened him.

"It was daunting," he reported. "It was like my son was not really there. He was shouting and baring his teeth. It was like one of those horror movies, only I was in the middle of it."

Houston told me that Mark paced shirtless and shoeless throughout the first floor of Vera's house, "like a caged animal." He hurled random threats at both of them, and, at one point, he gathered all the kitchen knives and began to swirl them in a threatening fashion.

He spat challenges at his father, "You think you're going to take me back, but you're not. We're going outside, and we're going to race up that hill. See that hill? And I'm going to win." He proceeded to knock objects off tables. Houston worried he would break something precious to Vera. Mark pulled books from bookcases and heaved them around the room and then made several piles with them. Houston and Vera became increasingly fearful.

"When I tried to touch him, he violently shoved me away," Houston said. "Mark seemed to move out of himself. I watched it happen! I was frightened for him, but I was really afraid for Vera and myself. I felt like Mark was holding us hostage."

As Mark became more viciously threatening with the knives, Houston gestured to Vera to call for help. "I really did not want to do that," he sighed. "But I didn't know what might happen next. I just knew Mark wasn't listening to anything we said."

When Vera called the local hospital, they told her to call 911. The second call brought a special unit of the Los Angeles Police Department (LAPD), the "psychiatric evaluation team." The special corps arrived within the hour, accompanied by uniformed officers with weapons drawn and eight cruisers. When Mark saw the swirling police lights, he seemed to sense danger for himself. He immediately ceased his threatening behavior and, clutching Vera's dog, fled to a nearby closet. Houston said, "It was amazing how fast he moved. It was as if he knew something bad was about to happen."

Mark hid in the closet until the police coerced him out. He remained confused and unclear about Houston's relationship to him. "I know you are not my father," he said at one point. "They sent you in his place, didn't they?"

Numbed by profound sadness, Houston recounted, "All I could do was put one foot in front of the other in order to keep going. I couldn't really think." He confessed that if he had stopped to process any of what he was seeing or hearing, he "would have been rendered helpless." Houston said to me, "You know, one of the most horrible times for me ever—one that tears at me whenever it comes to mind or wakes me in the night—is Mark being taken out of Vera's house in handcuffs. Like he was a criminal. He was bare chested, barefooted, and had on sweatpants she had loaned him. I just wanted to put my arms around him, that's all. They wouldn't even let me ride with him to the hospital."

In his rental car, Houston followed the police cruiser. The usual destination for LAPD psychiatric emergencies was County Hospital, but another caring friend in L.A. enabled Houston to get Mark processed through emergency into the UCLA Neuropsychiatric

Institute, a private facility. The private hospital was expensive. Houston held his breath and charged five thousand dollars on his credit card in order for Mark to receive care. It was financially difficult for us, but we wanted Mark to receive the best possible treatment. Before the close of Houston's second evening in Los Angeles, the UCLA Neuropsychiatric Institute admitted Mark as a patient. Mark was irate, verbally abusive, and uncooperative. He was held for seventy-two hours, the requisite time for emergency psychiatric evaluation, medication, and treatment. He spent a portion of those hours in four-point restraints.

The events of Houston's L.A. days played and replayed in his head. "On the way to the emergency room, I could see the back of Mark's head through the back window as I drove; he was sitting so straight. He never moved. I prayed he wasn't too scared," Houston told me.

He notified Lisa of Mark's whereabouts as soon as he reached the hospital. He was then fortunate to connect with another of our friends who cut short a business trip in Colorado to come to Los Angeles to lend a hand. When our friend, Craig, arrived, he and Houston met with Lisa. She recounted in detail Mark's previous few months. Lisa had been picking up the pieces of Mark's life as fast as they fell away. She provided excuses for his absences to his professors and university administrators. Since Mark could not focus sufficiently to read school assignments, she read pages aloud to him. She held his hand and rubbed his back whenever he became anxious or fearful. Sometimes she typed his papers into the night. "He just needs to stop smoking so much marijuana," she said. She refused to believe he was ill.

While Mark was in treatment at the UCLA psychiatric unit, his anger did not subside; he remained profoundly paranoid. He accused doctors and nurses of experimenting on him. He shouted that they were rough and unnecessarily hurtful. Doctors kept him restrained. Houston wanted to stay with Mark, to help pacify his raging son, but the hospital staff did not appreciate his presence. No one wanted Houston's account of the recent happenings. Brusquely, an intern told him to step outside the room. "You're making the patient anxious and irritable," he said. Mark told doctors that Houston was an enemy and not his father.

In spite of the signal to leave, Houston stayed on in L.A. He returned to the hospital the next day, hoping to speak with doctors about Mark's condition. He sat in the hallway near Mark's room, patiently waiting for a medical update. Doctors and staff passed him by without acknowledgment. He continued to sit. From time to time, he stepped into Mark's room to assure him that he was not alone. Finally, a resident assigned to Mark's case took Houston aside and said, "You need to leave. You need to go home to Philadelphia. Your son is bitterly angry with you. You continue to agitate him, and he says you abused him."

Houston reeled at the doctor's words: a "madman's lie," he told me softly. Based on Mark's stories, the doctor suggested that Houston seek a psychiatric evaluation. When Houston told me about Mark's accusation and the doctor's response, I was enraged. It took months for me to understand his eventual diagnosis of bipolar disorder and the impact it had on Mark's behavior. At that particular moment, I only knew that Houston needed me more than Mark.

Once Mark was able to recite his name, address, and other vital information, he was released from the neuropsychiatric institute at UCLA. The seventy-two-hour hold was at an end. Mark returned home to Lisa. He never filled his prescriptions for Depakote to curb his mood swings or his antipsychotic medication to stave off paranoia and delusion. He did not keep his appointments for psychotherapy. He returned to school at USC and found a job at a parking garage in Westwood Village. Years passed before Mark was well enough to apologize to his father for accusing him of abuse.

a father's return

OUR FRIENDS FROM NEARBY NEW JERSEY were with me when Houston arrived home from Los Angeles. They came in the morning, bearing delicacies from their local Whole Foods. While we waited, they made a lovely brunch in the sunshine of our backyard deck. I pushed food around my plate, not able to eat. When we heard the car in the driveway, a shadow of quiet fell over the afternoon, and my tears spilled over at the sound of Houston's voice. Mark was not with him. Our friends welcomed Houston home and quickly departed. Houston and I slipped into silence, not knowing exactly how to console each other. In four days, trauma had etched hard lines in his face. He was cryptic in his descriptions of Mark in the hospital. The details were too painful to surface. We were afraid to touch; we might never stop crying.

Little by little, Houston told me what had happened in Los Angeles. He described Mark's paranoia and his bouts of mania and depression. The medical center doctors diagnosed Mark with Bipolar Disorder Type I. Mark's habit of self-medicating with drugs and alcohol had complicated the disorder. He needed prolonged rest, psychotherapy, and medication. Unwilling to accept the hospital diagnosis, Mark returned to Lisa and resumed his previous lifestyle. Houston and I did not know much about mental illness, yet we had unknowingly witnessed some of Mark's symptoms of bipolar disorder.

At the urging of friends in the medical profession, Houston and I sought the help of a psychiatrist. Dr. Roth had a substantial caseload of clients with bipolar disorder. Although he had never met our son, he was able to teach us about the disorder and its complexities. In one office conversation, looking at each of us in turn, Dr. Roth asked, "And so, enough about Mark. How are *you* doing?" I began to tell him about my sleeplessness, and he interrupted me, "No, I mean how are the two of you doing as a couple?"

I was instantly silent. I knew I had been avoiding Houston, and he, me. Our conversations were usually about Mark. Things we used to enjoy doing, like planning a real summer vacation or having dinner parties with friends, were specters of the past. Taking a day off from work and sightseeing in Philadelphia had not really occurred to either of us. Houston and I simply worked and came home to prepare for the next day; sometimes Mark or Lisa called us from Los Angeles and that ended our evening.

Dr. Roth put Houston and me back in touch with each other as a couple. He told us what we could expect if we continued to send money to Los Angeles, gratifying Mark's requests. Other parents had reported bankruptcy. He told us our options were simple: "Wish him well and walk away, decide your limits and stick to them, or bring him home." If we continued to answer Mark's needs first, we could permanently damage our relationship. "You did not cause this illness," he said. "But you can make your lives miserable by throwing money after it. You are becoming enablers. Mark cannot understand that you are trying to help. At this point, he is feeding a habit."

Dr. Roth urged us to locate a parental support group and to start educating ourselves about mental illness. He had only a few success stories. He told us that rescue is not possible without the patient's full cooperation. He helped us accept long-term coping strategies for an illness that had no cure. Over the course of three years, Dr. Roth taught us to say no to a son whose difficulties and requests for money only escalated.

When Mark returned to his L.A. home after his medical treatment, he and Lisa picked up where they had left off. They resumed heavy drinking and drug use. Partying with friends was a weekly event even though Mark was still in school. Houston and I learned that Mark purchased marijuana whenever he could, usually with the money we provided for other things. Around this time, Mark described his manic moments this way:

I walk these streets,
elusive as a cat,
and sacrifice myself
for the city.
Chunks of my flesh
have rubbed off here,
blood-red as the brick
that tore them.
My skin's a dismembered jigsaw puzzle.
I am enlightened,
yet invisible,
brilliant and unseen.
Injured—
fluid motion.

Whenever Mark called us, we grew to expect his anger and accusations. It was easier to speak with Lisa since her requests were always clear and straightforward. She gave us unadorned reports of our son: "He's stressed out and drinking a lot. I think he's worried about his classes," she said. She refused to discuss illness, and she did not believe Mark suffered from bipolar disorder. She stood firm on that point.

Money was still the main point of contention in our phone calls, but I never said to Mark or Lisa, "There is no more money. Stop calling if you are only calling for money."

After spending more than we could afford and not seeing any of the money used for psychiatric treatment, Houston felt our contributions were unproductive.

"This is obviously not working. We've tried everything. Dr. Roth told us that sometimes you have to walk away. I love him too, but maybe he just needs to hit the bottom again. Maybe then he will ask for psychiatric help," Houston said.

I disagreed, saying, "Mark is ill. He has bipolar disorder. I know what Dr. Roth said, but how will we know when Mark needs help if we just let go?"

I certainly did not know which strategy might work, but I wanted to keep sending money to Los Angeles if it meant I could keep Mark in my sights. I was so afraid he would vanish.

Two weeks later, Mark informed us that he and Lisa were married. They had eloped to Las Vegas and exchanged vows in a small chapel on the strip. "It was a lark!" he said. After that call, we did not hear from Mark for months. The two of them simply disappeared. No telephone number worked. Our letters went unanswered. A few were returned with NO FORWARDING ADDRESS stamped across the front. Whenever I heard the telephone company recording, "This is no longer a working number," I told myself that Mark and Lisa had just not paid the phone bill. Sometimes, I even convinced myself I had confused the numbers while dialing and that I should simply call later. It was impossibly difficult for me to accept that I had no idea where Mark was living.

After a few months, Lisa called out of the blue, using "my friend's phone" and saying, "Mom, we could use some extra money. We need to turn the lights back on." I asked about Mark. She said he was fine. He was working. She gave no further information. "We don't have a phone right now," she offered during one of our uncomfortable pauses.

"Please, just call and give us your number when you get a phone," I begged.

She gave me a P.O. box number for the money and promised to stay in touch. Mark never called. Lisa never sent a telephone number. I mailed money for the electric bill. By October 1996, Mark and Lisa had vanished totally from our lives. Our son was a black man suffering from bipolar disorder; he was unmedicated, probably high, and often on the edge of rage. I could not bear to picture him wandering the streets of Los Angeles.

Houston and I were devastated by Mark's disappearance. We made every phone inquiry we could. We had friends calling friends. We grew increasingly depressed, even in the presence of each other. We talked little and filled the house with music to cover our silence. The only outings we made were routine grocery trips and visits to Dr. Roth. After our doctor appointments, we stopped to see friends who lived near the medical complex in Bryn Mawr. We gave them updates; they gave us tea. I remember going to bed each night, but I do not remember sleeping. I remember opening my eyes from time to time, checking the passing minutes on the digital clock. We slept wherever we happened to fall.

In my grief, I remembered one of Mark's poems. I wondered if he had written it during an earlier depression:

The sun shines bright tonight
on the other side of the world.
But it is dark where I lie
awaiting the dawn.

interlude

MARK CALLED IN JULY 1997. It had been almost one year since our last contact. Houston accepted the call. The cavalier tone of Mark's voice made it seem as if it had been only a few weeks.

"Hey Dad, I just called to tell you that you have a grandson! We named him Jack." Jack was four months old. We did not even know he had been expected.

Houston was not sure whether to be elated at the birth of his first grandson or even more elated to hear Mark's voice after so many months.

"Mark . . . Mark, is that you? Are you all right? Where have you been?" he stumbled.

"Dad, you have a grandson!" Mark replied, ignoring the questions. "Aren't you happy about that?"

Houston was more relieved than joyous. His own son was alive. Mark had held onto his parking garage job. Houston could hear him exchanging greetings with drivers as they passed through his cash-register exit lane. After Houston congratulated Mark on Jack's birth, Mark said, "OK, Dad, later!" and hung up the phone.

When Houston told me about his surprise phone call, he was clearly confused and unsettled. It was such momentous news. We made an effort to be happy. Houston and I telephoned friends, near and distant, just to hear the words spoken aloud: "We have a grandson!" We celebrated on our backyard deck, just the two of us. First-time grandparents, we toasted with champagne. Houston smoked an obligatory cigar, a gift from a neighborhood friend. We still did not know Lisa and Mark's telephone number or address.

We later discovered that Mark, Lisa, and Jack, the new baby, had moved from one living arrangement to another.

Gradually, they let us back into their lives. With his untreated bipolar disorder, Mark struggled to keep his minimum-wage job and maintain a family. Dodging and hiding, they avoided bad checks, debts, and bad credit. Mark was sick and just well enough to know it.

On a Sunday afternoon not long after Jack's birth, Mark, spiraling downward, flew into a manic rage. He wrecked the kitchen, unshelved everything in the refrigerator, threw furniture out the window, smacked Lisa as they tussled, and climbed half-clothed onto the fire escape to curse his neighbors and most of the rest of the world. Lisa had to call the Los Angeles Police Department three times before anyone responded. A lone cruiser appeared with lights flashing. According to Lisa, Mark was out of control because he drank too much alcohol. Mark insisted they argued all the time. This time, however, Lisa had bruises. Officers handcuffed Mark and shoved him into the cruiser. He was now in the hands of the law.

Much later, Mark reflected on this time of his life:

Suffocated with darkness before dawn
Marking time with illness.
I am captive of this manic cross.
Its shadow encases me
in confines of self-spun illusion.
I sleep in its box where
images surround me,
abundant as voices at

Broadway intermissions.
This madness
has lifted the burden of decision.

In Philadelphia, Houston and I received a frightening phone call. The recorded voice said, "This is a collect call from a correctional facility in Los Angeles, California. The rate is one dollar and ten cents a minute. Say 'yes' if you wish to accept this call from ["Mark," came the pronouncement of his name]."

Trembling, I uttered, "Yes." I remember saying, "I'm so sorry, Mark. What happened?"

I half listened to his story, all the while trying to figure out how to get him out. Then I heard him say that he had hit Lisa. That stopped me cold. We taught Mark never to hit a woman. My compassion grew weak.

Nobody in my immediate family had ever been in jail. My son had had every opportunity for success, yet he was now in jail. I was not sure what to say to my mother and father or to Houston's parents. Would my family think I had failed as a mother? I was so ashamed I could hardly speak about it.

Houston called his older brother, a well-respected lawyer with an extensive network of friends and colleagues. He came to our aid with sympathy and gave us the name of a first-rate Los Angeles criminal attorney. Unfortunately, this attorney's retainer was $10,000, more money than we had in any bank account. We used a newly secured credit card with a $10,000 limit. The lawyer was able to bail Mark out since his offense was a misdemeanor, but due to misplaced paperwork, Mark remained jailed for several more days after we posted bail. When he realized he had been held too long, Mark protested in writing. Using his lawyer's name, he requested immediate discharge. Because of the error, he would receive a government reimbursement check to cover missed workday wages. In reporting the situation to us, Mark said, "Lisa didn't check on me the whole time I was in here."

Lisa, however, had calmly told us, "I knew where he was. He needed to cool off."

After his release, Mark made his way back to their apartment, walking and hitching rides. When he got to the apartment, Lisa was not in a welcoming mood. The apartment was still thick with bad feelings. She had not cleaned up the aftermath of Mark's manic rampage. "I bought her flowers with some change I had in my pocket," he said. "But she never even turned around when I walked in."

In the days following Mark's return, he and Lisa argued constantly. The government reimbursement check arrived the second week. After a particularly intense feud, Mark made the hasty decision to leave. "I didn't want things to get out of control again," he told me later. "I knew I had to get a long, long way away. I knew I could not keep it together," he explained. "I was seriously ready to hurt myself or somebody else. I didn't know what was wrong, and it scared me. I had that check, so I left."

Lisa called us in Philadelphia when Mark had not come home for three days. She explained, "He came in from work, and he stayed a few minutes. Then he picked up a few things and left. We had only said a few words to each other when he grabbed his keys and said, 'I'll be back,' but I haven't seen him in days. I'm really worried. He's never stayed away this long, and he never stays away from Jack." Mark had taken their car. Lisa was worried, and I certainly was too. She did not usually call at times like this. Mark was missing in action once again, this time even from his L.A. family.

Later, a remorseful Mark wrote:

Hot tempered frowns
boil over
like pasta in unsalted water.

I have touched you again
without love,
injured your rocky emotions
tough as the hair follicles
that resisted being pulled,
as I begged for you
to tell me you loved me.

cop land

WE WERE NOW TALKING TO Lisa several times a week, suggesting options for her, Angela, and Jack, and sending extra money to help with our grandson. Houston and I were concerned about Jack's welfare. At the same time, we had complex feelings about being reeled in for money and then forcibly bounced out of Mark's life when we were no longer needed. Reciprocity was nonexistent. We had never met Jack, nor had we been invited to do so. It had been almost two years since Mark's call in distress and Houston's attempt at rescue. Once again we faced the recurring question, *What should we do?* Perhaps we needed to go to Los Angeles after all. Could our son still be wandering around without medication and treatment? One night after turning off the light, I could hear Houston sobbing quietly. He tried to lie still, but I could sense his wakefulness.

When Mark disappeared this time, it was Houston who knew he was coming home. One Friday evening, I announced, "We are not going to cook tonight. We're going out on a date! And one rule: We will not talk about Mark the entire evening."

Houston, amused, raised his eyebrows and said, "That's different." We had become reclusive, dodging invitations from friends with lame excuses, creeping ever deeper into despondency.

Trying to sound upbeat, I continued, "Tonight we're going to a movie, and you get to choose! We'll just eat hot dogs and popcorn like we used to and mindlessly follow the plot. Nothing more. I'll drive. OK?" Houston thought for only a second and accepted my invitation. I chose a theater about an hour away. It seemed more like a date that way.

As I was driving, Houston off-handedly commented, "I have just one more thing I need to say about Mark, and then I'll stop."

"That's not what we agreed on!" I protested.

"Just one thing," he continued. "I want you to know so that you won't be upset when it happens." I steeled myself.

He said quite simply, "Mark is coming home." Not looking my way, he continued, "I don't know how I know; I just know."

Houston did not make such comments. I was usually the one who ventured pronouncements like that. He seemed so sure of himself. His words and affect rattled me. I thought the strain and pressure had finally gotten to my husband. I hoped I was not losing another man in my life. It was absurd to think that Mark could get from California to Philadelphia; he had absolutely no money. I blocked out Houston's revelation and drove on to the movie. We definitely needed time away from home. Houston's mind, however, was working overtime; he chose a movie about police and violence, *Cop Land*. Nevertheless, with popcorn and sodas, the evening proved the most fun we had had in months.

As they had so often, my thoughts before sleep that night went straight to Mark. During his childhood and teenage years, he and I marveled at our near telepathy. So I tried sending a mind message to him as I had done so many times in the past: *Be safe, Mark, wherever you are.* Then, I gave myself permission to relax. I put disaster on the back burner and slipped into a deep sleep.

It seemed only minutes later that Houston was calling me, "Charlotte! Come down. Come down, now." It was morning. His voice was far away but urgent. It was a brilliantly sunny day in August. Was I dreaming? I fought the haze of sleep and fatigue. We always let each other sleep late on weekends. Why was he calling me?

After I playfully acknowledged him, he said more insistently, "You've got to come now!" When I got to the top of the stairs and looked down, Houston was at the front door in his bathrobe, looking through the glass.

"What is it?" I asked over the upstairs banister. Houston did not turn around.

"Mark is home," he said matter-of-factly. I immediately recalled Houston's uncanny disclosure from the previous night. "There's a taxi," he said to the closed door.

"That can't be true," I murmured.

I rushed into my bathrobe and splashed water on my face, trying to jolt an unwilling body into wakefulness. I heard Houston ask, "What do you need, son?"

"Money for the cab," Mark replied.

As I reached the hallway downstairs, all I could do was stare. Mark was unkempt and dirty. He was unable to make eye contact with me. I knew he was ill.

"Mark, how did you get here? Where have you been? We've been so worried," I bombarded him with questions.

"Mom, stop!" he said, turning abruptly. "Aren't you going to say hello? That you're glad to see me?"

The ugly truth is I was not glad. I was frightened. He was unrecognizable, this man in my hallway, calling me "Mom." He was emaciated. His clothes hung on his frame. He looked and smelled of old smoke, sweat, and days on the road. His longish hair was disheveled, and he needed a shave. At first glance, he seemed to have a huge gap in his front teeth. Upon closer scrutiny, I realized his teeth were horribly stained, the result of cigarettes and too much coffee. This man was worn, as if he had been homeless for weeks.

When his indomitable dimples showed through in a sunken grin, I saw Mark. I reached out to touch him but drew back when I realized his body was quivering ever so slightly. Houston and I stole glances at each other as we stood uncomfortably in the middle of our sunlit hallway that August morning. Then it was as if someone yelled, "Action!" Like automatons, we moved to separate destinations. Houston, in dazed slow motion, said to Mark, "Let's find some clothes for you. How about a shower?" He was so very kind to our son, as if a needy stranger had just happened by.

Bewildered, I took the cue and ordered myself to respond in similar fashion. "You must be hungry. I'll fix you something to eat." I felt like the mother in a TV ad, artificial and rehearsed.

Houston whisked Mark off to the back of the house. As they moved from the hallway, I became aware that Mark was clutching a small, navy-blue gym bag. That's all he had. I asked gently if he had clothes in the bag. His answer was curious and abrupt; "No, it's just a teddy bear and a doll."

"Why?" I asked.

"It's Jack's favorite bear and a new doll for Angela," he responded. "I brought them with me so when I go back home, they will remember who I am."

I was both taken aback and moved by his response. I nodded as if I understood.

When Houston took our son off to shower and dress on that Saturday morning in 1997, I grabbed the telephone directory, headed to a side room, and started dialing emergency numbers. I needed a doctor, an agency, anybody who could advise me how to help our son. He was obviously very sick. It was the end of summer in Philadelphia, and each of the doctors I called had a vacation message on the answering machine. I called our local hospital emergency room. The first questions the psychiatric nurse asked me were, "Are you afraid? Are you in danger?"

"Should I be afraid?" I asked him. The nurse's very suggestion of danger unsettled me.

"Anything could happen," he replied.

I told him Mark was not a problem. He answered, "You need to call 911 if he becomes violent. Be sure to tell them how he's behaving. Good luck." That was the extent of his information and advice. I held onto the receiver long after the call had ended.

During the evening, I could hear Mark pacing down the hall and mumbling to himself. Before I went to sleep, for the first time ever, I locked our bedroom door.

The next morning, momentarily forgetting Mark's arrival, I awakened with a line from one of his poems running through my mind: "Me? I will love you until God dies." He had sent it to me seven months prior. This is the poem Mark wrote for his firstborn son who, Mark said, "kept me alive":

> Me?
> I will love you until God dies.
> Your eyes' innocence
> teaches me beauty in simplicity
> and depth in newness.
> With a glance you spell my worth,
> make my heart rejoice at knowing
> that each beat now has reason
> and meaning.
> When this life is through,
> we will embrace, hold hands,
> laugh again together
> under always clear skies,
> and love one another
> until God dies.

I smiled. Then I stretched fully awake and remembered Mark's presence in my house. Was he awake? Was he still roaming the hallway? Suddenly, I was on my feet.

madness on vacation

I HEARD MARK SHOWERING IN the bathroom below. He alternated between singing loudly, out of tune, and talking to someone in loud whispers. He was not addressing his father, and there was no one else in the house. My jaw tightened. Then I heard Houston moving about in the kitchen, and I heard low mumbling exchanges as Mark entered. When I joined the two of them in the kitchen, it was clear Mark had slept little. He spoke in a steady stream of non sequiturs, making emphatic gestures with his hands. I could not follow what he was saying. He began to pace the floor. It was only Sunday morning; we had another full day to wait before we could visit with a doctor. A psychiatrist friend had called in a prescription that would calm Mark's anxiety until she evaluated him first thing Monday morning. I had to think of a diversion for the day, something to distract everyone.

Houston and I decided to find a K-Mart and take Mark shopping for clothes. Mark had brought nothing with him. K-Mart was inexpensive and practical; it had been our usual shopping place when Mark was growing up. The idea of venturing out into public seemed a good one. I thought Mark's erratic behavior would not be so evident in a crowd. When we arrived at the local K-Mart, however, we soon realized that in the flow of a bustling store, Mark was extremely uncomfortable. He glared at passersby and turned around to follow them until they broke his gaze and fled. I kept walking and talking, hoping Mark would keep pace and engage in one of the topics I suggested for conversation. Nothing interested him. I could see him begin to deteriorate as we moved through the store. Mark began to sneak down aisles where

I could not see him, not in a teasing or kidding manner, but actually to hide. When I smiled and cajoled, asking if he was trying to find something, he shouted, "Does it look like I'm trying to find something? Can't you see them staring at me?" Nearby shoppers glanced our way and then quickly left the space. I hurried our clothing selection.

In the course of our shopping, a man accidentally brushed me with his cart. I said, "So sorry," and we exchanged quick apologies. Mark darted between us, his eyes flashing back and forth. He was tensed for battle.

"Did you touch her?" he demanded. His face had an eerie, menacing grin; he seemed prepared to strike. "Did you touch my mother? Did you?"

The young black man to whom he spoke was not intimidated. "No," he stated. They stared at each other, both unafraid, ready to come to blows in K-Mart.

"Mark, it really is OK. I'm fine," I insisted. "He just passed by me. It's really OK." I was able to convince Mark that I was not hurt, but the two men continued to stare.

Needing to regroup after K-Mart, Houston and I decided to stop for a quick meal at T.G.I. Friday's before returning home. It had been one of Mark's favorite neighborhood restaurants. We thought we could blend in with the crowd. Mark had not eaten all day and had to be ravenous. I had been wondering when the medicine Mark had taken that morning would finally start working and subdue him to some degree or even put him to sleep. But Mark talked nonstop. We watched his every move, and he watched us. When the server came to take our orders, it was obvious that Mark could not read the menu. At the time, we did not realize he had damaged his eyes staring into the sun. He had been "looking for God." High on grass, he thought he could "become one with the sun." As he described it:

It is a sunny day. I am at home smoking marijuana with my using partner and wife. She always did roll up good. It seems like the joint has been passed back and forth at least a dozen times. Suddenly, the filter is lifted and everything is instantly amplified. Colors are brighter than usual, sounds louder. Thoughts race through my mind like motorcycles at top speed. It's all kind of strange and more than a little uncomfortable. By the time the joint is finished, I feel close enough to God to look Him directly in the eye. I look directly into the sun without blinking. I burn holes in both of my retinas.

We read the menu and ordered for him. When his meal arrived, Mark lowered his head down to the table and shoved food into his mouth, barely stopping to breathe and swallow. We gazed in disbelief, trying not to stare.

When we reached home, Houston and I were exhausted. To our dismay, Mark was not tired at all. His mind had calmed somewhat, but not his body. Houston suggested that they shoot a few baskets in the driveway to burn off some of Mark's energy. Little did Houston know they would be there for two hours with Mark executing shots he had learned from playing basketball on the streets of L.A. and watching the NBA on television. His exuberance and excitement seemed unlimited. From the kitchen, I could hear Mark's shouts of "Play like a big man!" as he coached himself, dribbling and bouncing, making intricate moves toward the basket.

As he played, Mark spouted a continuous string of bizarre stories that Houston recounted to me the next day. Mark had narratives about his "army in Los Angeles" and the "lieutenant I left in command" when he traveled to Philadelphia. Houston served only as ball retriever, spectator, and listener. The late afternoon sun was wretchedly hot, so Houston suggested they take a break to shower and get a cool drink. Instead, Mark challenged his father to a run in the park, "to clear out the lactic acid from the basketball." Finally, Houston was able to persuade him to sit on the back deck.

Mark's energy was boundless. Later, we learned to identify this as mania.

I joined Mark and Houston for a bit of small talk and then made apologies, escaping to the safety of my bedroom. I thought Houston would soon follow. An hour later, I could still hear the soft strains of the backyard radio and the continuous hum of Mark's voice; Houston had not moved from the deck for fear of upsetting him. Mark told him bizarre stories about strange creatures who systematically deposited dead bodies in a room near his apartment in L.A. and a man who had been drugged by secret agents so that he could only see the world in cartoon fashion. Houston listened until early morning dew wet the grass of our backyard.

three

struggling to heal

MARK WAS HOME. HE FLED to us because he had nowhere else to go. We accepted him without question. Now what?

As soon as he was situated in his old room, Mark became obsessed with finding work. Houston and I were preoccupied with one thing only: finding a suitable doctor for our son to begin psychiatric treatment. Houston and I thought hospitalization was the answer to getting Mark treatment, but as I made calls to various hospitals and rehabilitation units, we learned that no psychiatric hospital would ever admit Mark in his present state. His moods were unstable, but he was not "a danger to himself or others," the criterion for psychiatric hospital admission. Furthermore, Mark had no psychiatrist to refer him. Blocked at all turns, I realized we were Mark's only resource. We became, in effect, Mark's unofficial legal guardians. Our home became his rehabilitation facility.

I continued making calls, seeking referrals from doctors and advice from friends in Philadelphia about possible treatment facilities. Our psychiatrist friend agreed to provide Mark with maintenance medication and therapy until we found a doctor specializing in mood disorders. In our friend's medical opinion, Mark's psychiatric condition was complex, volatile, and potentially dangerous if not treated. She explained that Mark would need psychotherapy for an indefinite period. In time, we found a highly respected specialist in bipolar disorder. His office was a forty-minute drive from our home, and one of us drove Mark there three times a week.

Mark was miserable and dispirited. He knew he needed help, but he had no idea what that would involve. Mark also hated being away from Lisa and the children. Every day, he phoned Lisa in

California, encouraging her to relocate to the East Coast. Lisa's aunt, who lived in Atlanta, Georgia, eventually invited Lisa, Jack, and Angela to come and share her home. Before Thanksgiving that year, Lisa and the children traveled by Greyhound bus from L.A. to Atlanta, periodically checking in with me by telephone as they traveled across the country. Mark and Lisa held onto the idea that Mark would eventually join them in Atlanta. He told us repeatedly, "I have a family. I have to get back to my family."

Silently, I thought, Aren't we your family? You came to us. Remember?

Mark writes of his loneliness:

Sometimes,
I dream lucid and clear landscapes,
Framed by shallow streams,
And trees fit for climbing.
Sometimes, I dream,
Of death being none of these things,
And weep

I see their smiling faces,
Feel their touch,
And wonder if
I cherish moments enough.

Mark's new psychiatrist, Dr. G., prescribed sleep, rest, and three types of medication to treat his bipolar disorder: Depakote, Risperdal, and Seroquel. For about a month, Mark's symptoms of mania and psychosis persisted. He slept little and talked to people we could not see. As the month passed, we watched the signs of madness diminish. We no longer heard Mark talking to himself, flying high with mania. However, as the prescribed medication began to work, Mark experienced side effects: fitful sleeping, poor memory, a shuffling gait, dry mouth, unblinking eyes, and shaking hands.

Mark spent about three weeks acclimating to the effects of the medication. He told us that his doctor advised him to rest as much as possible. "How am I going to do that and still look for a job?" he worried. I consoled him by saying that he had to get well before moving ahead. First and foremost, Houston and I were concerned that Mark follow his doctor's advice, and I asked Mark if he would allow us to talk with his doctor about his treatment.

I was relieved when Mark agreed, "I guess you should know what's going on. I do see you more than I see the doctor. I'll ask Dr. G. if it's OK." For the next appointment, Mark's doctor invited Houston and me to sit in on part of the session.

Houston and I explained our commitment to Mark's wellness but said we were confused about how to help him.

His doctor nodded. "It is confusing," he agreed. "Mark thinks he should be working, but he needs as much rest as possible in order for his brain to heal."

"How long will he be taking the medication you prescribed?" Houston asked.

"Mark will be taking some form of medication for the rest of his life in order to treat his bipolar disorder," Dr. G. answered matter-of-factly. "We will have to try different combinations until we find the one best suited for him. For a while, it will be trial and error. We need patience."

Mark was sitting near me, and I could feel him tense up when Dr. G. said "patience." I spoke quickly to preclude an interruption from Mark.

"Mark is applying for jobs now, and he hopes to find one soon. Is this feasible?" I asked.

"He can work, but only if it is not too stressful. His hours need to be short," Dr. G. answered emphatically.

I continued to describe our situation: "Mark tells us every day that he has to go to Atlanta to be with his wife and children. I feel his urgency, Doctor. Given his present condition, when do you think he might be able to join them in Atlanta?"

Dr. G. did not speak right away. He looked at Mark and then at each of us and said, "I would not say that Mark is ready to go to Atlanta anytime soon. I think Mark knows that if he leaves before his therapy is further along, he will relapse. We've talked about this."

The three of us left the doctor's office in distress. Houston and I felt sad for our son. Had he known about the need for medication for the rest of his life? The news shocked us. It must have shocked him, as well. When I look back on that moment, I realize how naïve we were at the time and how little Houston and I knew about bipolar disorder.

Later that evening, Houston and I discussed the morning session with the psychiatrist. We had needed to hear from the doctor what was happening with our son, and we needed to know the extent of his treatment. We wanted to understand our part in his recovery. We were both very angry that the meeting had been so long in coming and that we were the ones finally to ask for it. I was agitated: "How could a doctor begin to understand how to treat Mark's illness without hearing what we have to say? He doesn't have a clue about Mark's behavior toward us. He didn't even ask us if Mark was taking his medicine!"

Houston wrapped his arm tightly around my shoulders. I felt more empty and angry than I had before the meeting. I asked Houston, "Did you know this was only the beginning? Did you know that Mark would be sick forever?"

Mark began to look for a part-time job. The effects of his new medication prevented him from driving, so he traveled by foot or public transportation in order to submit applications. He found this especially disturbing. Mark is a good driver. In Los Angeles, he was used to navigating freeways.

Early one afternoon, Mark set out for the Chestnut Hill shopping district not far from our Lafayette Hill home and invited me to come along. I window-shopped while Mark went inside a card shop to submit a job application. I saw him smile broadly and shake hands with the store manager. They chatted for a few minutes, and Mark walked out empty-handed. With a half smile, he said, "Not this one." When Mark went into the next shop, a hardware store, I saw customers glance his way as he held out the completed application form for the manager. They saw what I saw: Mark's shaking hands.

I watched the manager take the paper and smile. I knew this would be an instant rejection. He told Mark, "Thank you. I'll hold onto this just in case we get an opening. I'll give you a call."

By midafternoon, Mark's eyes were beginning to droop. He had submitted four job applications. Walking the avenue and asking for jobs was a new routine for both of us. I marveled at Mark's perseverance.

Mark never gave up on finding a job. He combed the classified ads looking for labor that would yield money to send to Lisa, her daughter, and Jack. He told one of our neighbors, "I'll work at anything for pay." He tore out one ad that read, "Long distance truck drivers needed." He filled out the application and went off alone on public transportation to turn it in. When Mark returned, Houston explained gently to him that truck driving was not a plausible job opportunity. Houston reminded Mark of his doctor's instructions that driving was not possible until his medication was properly adjusted.

"But long distance is good money," Mark protested.

"I know, Mark. But long distance drivers don't get much sleep either," Houston responded. Mark's fantasy was short-lived.

His next idea was to join the military. We listened.

"I know I'd make a good recruit," he said to us one evening. "I have the education, and I want even more. That's what they're looking for!"

He was revved up; he met with a recruiter and applied. The recruiter was extremely delighted to meet someone like Mark. Mark told me later, "I knew I was almost in, Mom. I could tell by the interview. And then I had to fill out papers about my health history. I could have lied, and I would have been in," he said shaking his head. "I just couldn't do it. I couldn't lie."

The following week, Mark found and accepted a job at a box company, accessible by public transportation. The job required him to lift and then break down heavy boxes and crates almost equal to his own weight. Mark was still underweight, and the job was physically exhausting. Houston and I saw him drag in from work, barely able to eat. We urged him to quit, and, reluctantly, he did.

Mark took a little time off to recuperate and then resumed his job search. One evening, as I prepared our dinner, I realized Mark had not yet returned. It was getting dark, and we became very uneasy. He was usually home before nightfall. "I'm going to Chestnut Hill to look around. He should be home by now," Houston said. His voice sounded worried. He grabbed his keys and headed for the car.

His first stop was the old trolley turnaround where Mark's bus let off all passengers. Then Houston walked to Germantown Avenue and stepped in and out of shops, looking for Mark. "I was so concerned that he was sick somewhere. I kept thinking the worst," he told me.

As Houston was driving back, he spotted Mark walking slowly toward home. He pulled over and rolled down the window. "Get in. I was worried about you. What happened? You're so late," he said.

Mark was unruffled. "I just thought I'd walk around some and stop in the drugstore to check out the magazines."

"But it was getting dark," Houston persisted. "We didn't know where you were. You're always back before dark."

Exasperated, Mark sighed, "Can't I have any freedom? You're always breathing down my neck, telling me what to do!"

I heard only one car door slam when they returned. Houston waited in the car to gather his thoughts. Mark ignored me as he brushed past the kitchen door and headed for his room. Later at dinner, I saw fatigue in his face. He then reached under the table and pulled up a shopping bag. He gestured to both of us, saying, "Happy anniversary, you guys. I stopped today and got you something. Not much."

I let out the breath I was holding in and said, "Mark, thank you so much. This is so thoughtful! Wow!" My heart lightened.

I looked at Houston, and his eyes were brimming with tears. He sprang to his feet with arms outstretched and gave Mark a bear hug, saying, "Thanks so much, Mark!"

Houston and I both had forgotten it was our anniversary. Mark's gift was a commemorative edition of *Life* magazine, celebrating the 1960s in black-and-white photographs. I was moved that Mark remembered how much I enjoyed photography.

looking for work

MARK WAS VERY EMBARRASSED BY the side effects of his medication. He even created a phrase to describe his unblinking eyes: *the something-is-wrong-with-me stare.* One evening, as Houston gave Mark his pills, Mark looked at him and said, "You know you're poisoning me." Mark tossed his head back and swallowed. Although I knew the pills were helping Mark manage his bouts of mania, psychosis, and aural hallucinations, secretly I empathized with his viewpoint.

One hot afternoon, Mark and I strolled the hill together, still job searching. He would not give up. Mark was drawn to the cool interior of a high-end antique store. I went in with him, looking around on my own as he waited for the owner. Mark planned to ask if the store was hiring. I noticed, however, his preoccupation with the antiques on display. The way he touched them made me nervous. I was worried someone might see him as a threat; he was not browsing from a distance like the other customers. In this expensive shop, Mark moved his hands slowly, gently, along the smooth surfaces of a Chippendale breakfront. The furniture was shiny, attractive, and unaffordable. Mark's lips were curled slightly in a playful manner. The owner greeted him and asked if he needed information on any of the furniture pieces. Mark replied, "I do. You have gorgeous furniture. I am thinking of the breakfront. What's the price?"

The owner told him the cost, $12,000, and then gave Mark his business card. He suggested Mark return when he had given the purchase some consideration. Mark shook the owner's hand briskly and gave a parting nod. Mark was utterly charming. I found the whole thing strange. As we stepped out of the store, Mark said to me with a slight smile, "Did you see that?" I could not tell if he had been behaving theatrically (as he often liked to do) or if he was being manipulative. He seemed to enjoy the fact that he had duped the owner.

Houston and I knew that Mark needed money and that it was challenging for him in his present state to find work. Houston suggested that Mark do yard work for us during the summer. Since we had neglected the upkeep of our surrounding yard, I thought it was a good solution. We offered Mark eight dollars an hour and the chance to set his own schedule, resting as he needed and working when he wanted. We asked him to think of a design for the overgrown, scraggly yard on the side of our house. We told him we wanted a pathway connecting the front yard to the back. He liked our idea and asked if Houston was going to help him. That was not the plan. Houston said, "I'll get you started. I can't do it always. That's why we're hiring you." Without other work, Mark accepted the deal.

Following the doctor's prescription, Mark worked only a few hours each day, under minimal stress. We made a list of things we needed him to do: raking, pulling up weeds, tearing out old hedges, and preparing the ground for grass and flowers. When he began to tackle the jobs on our list, Mark could barely manage. He was underweight and suffering the side effects of his medication. He tired so quickly. I saw him sitting under a tree in the yard one afternoon, his head bowed. The summer heat and humidity did not help. He could only work two hours before his arms and legs ached. In early evening, Houston joined Mark in the yard, thinking that working together would energize Mark and help to keep him going. At the end of the day, however, work only made Mark more agitated and put him on edge.

One rainy evening, Houston suggested that the two of them try exercising for a bit. Houston thought that getting fit would help Mark feel better about himself. Mark was not only frail and adjusting to his medicine, but he was also getting used to the absence of alcohol and drugs. Mark jogged laboriously on the treadmill in our basement, but not for long. When I heard the slowing down of the machine, I remembered a time when he could run at top speed for twenty minutes of pure joy. On this rainy day, he lifted a few light weights and joked around with his father. It was good to hear them enjoying each other. In the past, they had loved working out together. Mark seemed in better spirits when they ascended from the basement. On exercise days, the dinner table was easy.

Mark gradually became stronger and even gained a few pounds. In his childhood, he had been even-tempered, and I noticed that his pleasant demeanor was slowly returning. I asked Mark how he was feeling one morning, and he answered amiably, "Not bad. At least my hands have settled down a bit." The doctor had adjusted Mark's medication, and his hands shook less.

About four months after his first meeting with Dr. G., Mark decided he was ready to submit more job applications. He and Houston agreed to finish the side yard on the weekends. "That pathway is mine!" Mark smiled, pointing definitively to the new white stone pathway from the front of the house to the back. I saw his pride, and, for a moment, I recognized someone who was beginning to look like my son.

The following week, Mark answered an ad from a bookstore about five miles from home. He traveled by bus and had no trouble finding the shop, Encore Books, tucked inside a small strip mall.

"The manager seemed nice, but she watched me like a hawk," Mark said when I asked how the interview had gone. "There were a lot of people applying, and we had to take a literature quiz. Can you believe it?" he continued. "Also, I was lucky I knew how to work a register. One guy didn't."

"Well, you probably did OK on the quiz, don't you think?" I asked. Mark shrugged his shoulders, as if it meant little.

As we were eating dinner that evening, the telephone rang. Mark immediately jumped up, saying, "That's Lisa." He grabbed the phone and took it into another room. We heard the agitation in his voice. Occasionally, we caught a word or sentence: "OK, OK! I'm doing the best I can." "I'm trying." "No, that's all I got!" Lisa called collect every evening; Mark accepted the charges. It was our telephone bill. We asked him, nicely, if he could keep their calls to two a week. He protested, "That's my family! I *have* to talk to them!" Later, Mark came into the television room, stuck his head in the doorway, and said, "Sorry I yelled."

Two days after Mark's bookstore interview, the manager called to say she wanted to hire him for a part-time position. Mark was elated. He picked up the phone to call Lisa but stopped abruptly and looked in my direction, "Is it OK?"

"Of course, Mark," I said.

He would start his real job the following week.

Mark's days were orchestrated; Houston and I decided what he could and could not do. He could not use our cars. We limited his long-distance calls. For many months, we kept and dispensed his medication. We thought he might not remember to take them and feared that he might, even in our presence, only pretend to swallow. Houston and I were dedicated to Mark's wellness. Whatever we needed to do, we did. I turned my face away from him when he dragged his feet into a room. I did not want him to see me crying. It pained me to watch him swallow pills and to see his heavy-lidded eyes, even though he clearly needed the medication. In eight weeks' time, Mark had ceased being manic, staying up all night, and telling nonsensical stories as if they were real. Each day we could see him come down to earth a little more.

Every morning, Houston or I awakened Mark for work. Often the medicine in his system drove him into a sleep that no alarm clock could penetrate. At least two or three times a week, he was hungover from his bedtime medication. When he awakened to snow and ice outside his bedroom window, he was tempted many mornings not to get up. Houston and I had to get to work ourselves, but on particularly wet and icy mornings, I drove a few extra miles to deliver Mark to the bookstore. Most days, he had to fend for himself, walking about a mile to the bus stop. He was then at the mercy of unpredictable urban transportation. I worried constantly that Mark would not get to work on time, if at all. If he lost this job, we knew it would be difficult for him to find another.

Although Mark's health was improving and he had finally found employment, our family life together was suffering. In the face of Mark's illness, Houston and I lost the ability to joke or even listen objectively to each other. With our son's return, incivility settled in to stay. We did not shout at each other but had started bickering, sometimes unknowingly, in public. Before turning in one night, we tried to decide how much money to give Mark for a week. He was now working part-time in the bookstore, but I felt he needed some money in his pocket for incidentals. Houston did not agree.

"He's getting paid every two weeks," Houston pointed out. "He's a man. Let him spend his own money for magazines and cigarettes. We're paying for his food and medicine and everything else. Lisa can send him extra change. She's working."

I answered with quiet frustration, "Houston, they don't have anything. That's why they argue. We have to help them in more substantial ways."

"We are already helping them," he shot back.

His abruptness annoyed me, and I replied, "OK, so what do you propose? Should we give him a regular amount each week like an allowance, or should we just give him a few dollars every now and then?"

Mark received a small check every two weeks. The bookstore job gave him a sense of purpose but little money. I held my ground, and, ultimately, Houston changed his mind. We finally decided to give Mark small amounts of money at random times, not to exceed $300 a month. With this arrangement, we were not offering to support Mark or to subsidize him so regularly that he could quit his bookstore job. Houston and I were both satisfied. One afternoon, I passed along twenty dollars to Mark and suggested he treat himself to a CD. Another time, Houston merely said, "Here's a little something to help the month along." Mark was pleased.

the family falters

MONEY WAS NOT OUR ONLY problem. I worried about Houston; I felt that we were not on the same page. Houston seemed unable, or unwilling, to acknowledge that our son was mentally ill. I think I accepted Mark's bipolar disorder and his addiction long before Houston did. At that moment in time, Houston half believed that Mark chose to drink and to take drugs and that Mark himself had brought on his own illness. Houston felt that Mark could pull it all together if he decided to. He found it too horrible to accept that Mark's problem stemmed from a disorder for which there was no cure.

Houston and Mark also quarreled. One evening, Houston and I were tired of listening to the music booming from Mark's room. Houston said to Mark as they passed in the hallway, "You need to shut your door. It's a mess in your room, and it smells. Your music is much too loud."

Mark was bleary-eyed. He stopped, tensed, and shouted back over his shoulder, "What's it to you? You don't live in my room!"

Houston answered sternly but calmly, "This is my house. If you don't want to play by my rules, you can leave."

Mark did not move. "Fuck that," he said to no one in particular.

"Where's your respect, Mark? You don't talk that way in our house!"

Trying to disengage their trigger switches, I cut in, "Houston, you're taking all this the wrong way. It's not that big a deal. Mark was not cursing at you."

Then I heard Mark snap, "Mom, just stop it! You can't 'make nice' out of this shit."

I stepped aside.

Later, Mark recalled his feelings of loneliness in our house, and he shared this poem:

Wilted sunflowers frame a
lone blue jay
in
fields of naked vision . . .

. . .wings,
spread,
now and again,
so the bird may
hover
(lest it forget,
amongst
such loss,
freedoms
of flight).

We moved ever so carefully around one another, but we could not seem to skirt the anger. It was clear we needed a third party to intervene. Mark had Dr. G., and I returned to Dr. Roth. Houston joined me. As Houston and I talked during our joint therapy session, we realized we were not inching a single step forward. We were at odds as to whether Mark should continue to stay with us and where he might go if he left. We had no idea if he would survive if he left Philadelphia. Houston and I believed that even our long-standing friends could not help us with the difficult, personal decisions we were facing, and, as such, we told no one what we were going through as a family. We did not know anyone who had been in our situation.

Houston and I discussed renting an apartment nearby for Mark. "He could come to our house for meals," I suggested, but then I remembered that Mark needed someone to oversee his medication and monitor his comings and goings.

"This cannot be happening!" Houston exclaimed. "I feel like we're a ship, and we're going down."

When Mark was a teenager, I used to accompany him and Houston on many of their movie outings. We have always been a movie family. On one such outing to see *Die Hard*, I became taken with Bruce Willis's besieged police character, who urges himself to "Think! Think!" I liked the notion of self-reminding, and it became my own mantra: "Think, Charlotte, think!" I realized that Mark and Houston had become enemy combatants who needed to be kept apart, and so I said, "You know, Houston, it seems as if you and Mark are battling adolescent issues. But he's not some angry teenager. He's a grown man, and he's very sick. He's very confused." Houston offered no comeback, and I continued, "He's your son, and you're angry that he's sick. You're angry that you can't do anything to fix it. I'm so sorry about that."

When I looked up, Houston was crying. I reached for him, and we held onto each other. We cried ourselves into a state of stuttered words. With dripping noses, we searched frantically for a box of tissues. When I offered Houston a supersized roll of toilet paper, we both began to laugh.

Later, we sat back down to think and plan.

"You and I are hurting differently," I began. "It's just you and me, Houston. How are we going to deal with this impossible situation? We both love our son."

Then Houston stunned me by saying, "I could leave. I've been thinking about it a lot. Things are not working with us all together. I could go to the Poconos for a while."

We owned a family vacation home in the mountains of Pennsylvania. Although the house in the mountains was only an hour and a half away from Philadelphia, I had not pictured living apart from Houston. How would I manage things without him? Realistically, I knew I could handle Mark in day-to-day life. Mark and I were compatible and rarely quarreled. I just did not want to be without Houston in Philadelphia. I thought further. I had a visiting professor post at the University of Delaware, and Mark had a job at the bookstore, only a bus ride away. We would both be busy. By the end of our talk, I had agreed to try Houston's proposal: I would stay with Mark in Philadelphia. Houston would leave for the fall semester.

The logistics of Houston's leaving were not simple. He had no sabbatical from the university. We had never spent more than a winter weekend in our house in the Poconos and did not know whether the house was built for sustained winter use. In those days, the house was a wooden chalet with problematic insulation. By the time Houston got there and settled in, it would be late fall with winter soon to follow. We had to prepare for cold weather. Also, after thirty years of marriage, we had spent no more than a fortnight apart on any assignment. Suddenly we were facing a separation that had no timeline.

At the university, Houston asked his department chair for a leave of absence. She was gracious and understanding when he told her what was happening at home. Since the fall semester was about to begin, Houston and I started planning for his departure. We told Mark only that his father needed quiet, uninterrupted time to finish a book in progress. I proceeded to help Houston pack. We stockpiled clothing catalogues, looking for silk underwear and lined boots. We caulked windows in the vacation house and compared prices on current home-heating systems. A wood-burning stove is charming for a two-day weekend, but chopping wood and cleaning cinders for an entire winter season would be onerous and time consuming. We hired a home-heating expert to assess our needs. He installed a propane system in the house. During one of our trips, we discovered that mice had tunneled from the basement into our living area upstairs, the consequence of leaving the space unused. We spent subsequent weekends cleaning up the mess, and we set traps to prevent further infestation.

We made four trips to the Poconos getting things in order for what turned out to be a six-month sojourn. While we made day trips back and forth to the mountains, Mark stayed alone in Philadelphia. I called him regularly to be sure that he was OK. We always returned by nightfall.

Houston and I had enjoyed preparing the house for winter; the early autumn weather was crisp and sunny. As we cleaned and shopped for supplies, we never lost sight of our impending separation. With the last of our emergency funds, we leased an SUV to ensure the safety of Houston's round-trips to and from Philadelphia. As it turned out, there was little snow that winter. Most weekends, it was safe and easy for Houston to travel. Later, however, he encountered back-to-back ice storms and had to plan his mountain travel to coincide with the sun.

On our final trip, we planned to stay overnight. I had prepared meals for Mark with instructions for oven heating. Mark was not a stranger to living on his own, but it was his first time alone overnight in our house since his return to Philadelphia. I was uneasy. For some unfathomable reason, I thought my presence in the house could guarantee Mark's safety. I know now that caution was unnecessary. Mark knew Philadelphia better than I did, and his sense of responsibility was improving. Nonetheless, I worried: Will he take his medicine in the correct amount? Will he take a walk in the neighborhood and forget to lock the house? Who will he call if he needs help?

When I called him, I felt silly saying, "Just checking in. Is everything OK?" Hearing Mark's voice comforted me. The next day, Houston and I drove back to Philadelphia in the late afternoon. Except for music playing at low volume, we rode in silence. As we got close to home, Houston glanced my way and said, "You know I'm going to miss you."

alone in philadelphia

MIDWEEK, HOUSTON DEPARTED PHILADELPHIA FOR the Poconos. It was early September 1998. Immediately, Mark and I set up a household schedule to accommodate our respective jobs. Mark's workday was short, so I asked him to help with household tasks: washing breakfast dishes, straightening the kitchen and den, and picking up the newspapers and mail. As the days passed, I noticed Mark's willingness to help out around the house without negative comments. I asked him if he would set the table for dinner, and I would bring in the food. We ate almost nothing but takeout dinners that semester. KFC with coleslaw (a nod to vegetables) was a favorite, and I got special credit for bringing in crust and grease for dinner. Occasionally, we ate hamburgers from McDonald's. Once we carved out a routine, our day-to-day life became easier.

Mark's sense of personal responsibility increased. He began to dispense his own medication, and I no longer had to stand nearby to watch him swallow the pills. I wondered if Houston and I had been hovering too closely, micromanaging his life. I assured myself that it was because of our diligence and care that Mark had progressed to caring for himself.

From time to time, I asked Mark if he needed to renew his prescriptions. I reminded him about his work hours and the necessity of being on time. One morning, as I headed out to the car with all of my teaching paraphernalia, I remembered I had not awakened Mark for work. I rushed back into the house and found him still asleep. I shook him awake. Waking Mark had been Houston's job.

I missed Houston's presence in the house, and I missed hearing his voice. However, I did not miss Mark's shouts and Houston's retorts, and I did not miss the tension between Houston and me.

Houston and I talked one evening, and he asked, "How's Mark doing?"

"Mark's doing really well," I was happy to tell him. "You'd be proud. He's counting out his pills every evening and remembering to take them. Also, he's helping out with dishes and stuff around the house. He likes to have company when he's working. We're doing just fine."

I cringed a little after I finished speaking. I did not want Houston to feel that Mark and I had created nirvana in his absence, but I did want him to know how positively Mark was progressing. My worry was unnecessary.

Houston's voice was soft and easy. He responded to my description of Mark's improvement with a delighted, "Yes!"

I asked Houston about his writing, and he told me he had written ten pages, thinking they were superb, and then later deleted them all. He chuckled and said, "It's OK because I know I can start again tomorrow and not expect a call to pick up Mark at the doctor's office. Thank you so much for taking care of our son."

Our momentary silence was a mutual smile over the telephone. He said, "I miss you."

Two weeks later, Mark called his father to tell him about "my job at the bookstore." I could hear him giving his father a blow-by-blow description of his average day, and when I heard him chuckle, I relaxed. Mark seemed especially proud to tell his father how many customers he had served in one shift. The next weekend, Mark was delighted when he got home in the middle of the day and discovered Houston's Jeep in the garage. I, too, remember getting home early from Delaware, thrilled to see Houston's car.

One weekend when Houston was home and Mark did not have to work, they went to Home Depot (one of their favorite errands) to find new grilling utensils so we could cook out that evening. Houston told me they both had found driving together relaxing: "I think it's because we don't have to make eye contact," Houston laughed.

Grilling together was one of their remembered joys, and I was a fan of their burgers. Weather never stopped us from grilling. I enjoyed watching father and son slowly rediscover pleasure in their relationship. When Houston left Philadelphia one Sunday evening to return to the mountains, I was particularly aware of the overcast feeling that invaded the house. I think our time apart made our weekends together easier, but it was still difficult to watch Houston drive away.

As I drove into the garage one evening after a long day of teaching, Houston's absence hit me hard. I was especially tired, and my day had not gone well. When I stepped into the house, I heard Mark's blaring stereo. The bass pounding of rap assaulted my senses, and the entire first floor of the house was completely dark. I could barely see two feet in front of me. I became undone. I screamed, "Marrrk! Where are the lights? Turn on the lights! Where are you? Marrrk!"

By the time he appeared, I was breathless. He was unperturbed, not at all concerned. "What's the problem?" he asked groggily.

"I hate coming into a dark house. You know that!" I said. The outburst had been cleansing for me.

By the next evening, Mark and I were back on track. We never stayed annoyed at each other for long. We talked during dinner, and Mark was particularly animated in describing Eve, his bookstore manager. "She is so easy to talk to, Mom," Mark exclaimed. "We talked about reading and how she loves novels about family living. I told her my favorites were mystery and gore."

I nodded, miming interest, and Mark continued: "And can you believe this, Mom? Eve was a nurse before she went into the bookstore business—and not just a regular nurse. She was a psychiatric nurse and worked in a state hospital in West Virginia."

This seemed like the first extended conversation Mark had had with anyone other than Houston and me in months. His excitement made me happy. He ate a bit and then continued, "Eve told me she figured I was on meds because she saw my hands shaking so badly. She had seen that with patients at the mental hospital where she worked. I think that's why she hired me. She felt sorry for me," he explained.

I winced but said nothing. He caught my expression and replied, "That's OK, Mom. I don't care. I got a job!"

I later met Eve in person. I went into the bookstore one day to thank her for giving our son a job in spite of her suspicion that he might have a few problems. "I had seen that side effect in my patients," she told me. We exchanged telephone numbers in case of an emergency for Mark. When I stopped by a few weeks later, Eve suggested that Mark check with his doctor. She noticed Mark's extreme fatigue as a possible red flag. Once Mark reported Eve's observation to Dr. G., he lowered Mark's Depakote level by half.

Arriving home a few evenings later, I saw as I drove up to the house that it was nicely lit on the first floor. I pulled into the garage and noticed, gratefully, that the house was quiet. I walked upstairs and was surprised to find Mark standing in the kitchen doorway. He smiled and said, "Hi, Mom. How's it going?"

At once, I relaxed. Mark guided me into the kitchen, all the while pointing toward the kitchen table where he had arranged a pièce de résistance: a homemade chocolate cake, leaning to one side. Puzzled, I glanced at Mark for an explanation.

"It's for you, Mom. I baked it. I remembered it was your favorite."

It was such a special evening. For dinner we ate nothing but cake. There was only a sliver left the next morning.

As Mark and I sat in the den one evening, dozing to the television's hazy-blue light, Mark startled me by saying suddenly, "You know, I left all my good friends back in New York when I left for Los Angeles. It was pretty damn lonely out there." The sadness in his voice roused me.

"What're you talking about? I thought you liked L.A."

He explained how after a month in Los Angeles, he yearned for New York. He missed the clubs and the all-night parties. "By comparison, L.A. was dull," he said. "If I hadn't found Lisa, my life would have been horrible, totally boring."

After talking with Mark about his life in New York and Los Angeles and hearing him pine for Lisa, I realized that he had no friends in Philadelphia. Other than Lisa, he only had his father and me to talk with, and we had become his guardians. Mark moved within a circumscribed geography between the bookstore, our home, and the moderately comfortable office of Dr. G. When he arrived in Philadelphia, he had been unable to concentrate sufficiently to read or write. During the time he lived with us, he slowly began to write again. Much later, Mark wrote about the time he spent with us in Philadelphia. He wrote this meditation long before the films *Happy Feet* or *March of the Penguins* graced our screens:

> During my nine-month uninvited (and unwanted) stay at my parents' home, I imagined I was an Emperor Penguin. They are really real. Emperor Penguins live in extremely cold conditions; I was in the cold of the east coast. I'd left the warmth of home in L.A. And in my parents' home I felt grossly out of place and uncomfortably frigid. It was

cold there. I had the urge to kill. This attracted me to shiny, sharp metal objects and made me fantasize daily. I thought about the best weapons and the fatal martial arts moves I could use to permanently subdue an adversary. I satisfied this urge by landscaping my parents' entire front and backyards (but not without substantial help from my father who had not intended to landscape his yard). I spent hours, shirtless and sweaty, tearing at overgrown weeds and roots with my bare hands, madly beating and displacing dirt with a garden hoe, frantically digging with a hand shovel. The earth bore the brunt of my ire. I also had the urge to get high and stay high. How I wanted a "hit." And the noise in my head would not stop. I tried to sate my addict appetite by shutting the door to my room and blasting raunchy, hard-core hip-hop on a portable radio I'd borrowed from my mother. The mania and paranoia made me see people in my room, and I paced to find a way out. But I was not sick—just sick of being in that house.

Emperor Penguins travel over fifty miles to reach their breeding ground. Once there, the females lay their eggs and leave their mates to guard and incubate and give birth to a new self. That's what I was trying to do. The male penguins stand virtually still for weeks on end while carefully balancing the delicate eggs on the tops of their feet. They stand frozen and wait for the family's reunion. I felt like an Emperor Penguin. I was waiting. I was standing virtually still. I wanted to see my family. I was obliged to treat my recovery like a delicate egg. I missed my wife and my children, especially my four-month-old son, Jack.

I tried not to neglect my sanity, so I gingerly tried to balance things and make the distinction between delusion and reality, between nightmares and real life horrors. I struggled *hard to nurture some semblance of mental stability so I could meet with small forms of forgiveness, elation, and appreciation when I joined my wife and children. No one seemed to understand. I was an Emperor Penguin. Cold, a father . . . alone.*

At Thanksgiving, Mark made a bus trip to Atlanta to visit Lisa and the children for a long weekend. When he returned to Philadelphia, he worked diligently at Encore Books for another six months. As soon as Mark received his meager paycheck every two weeks, he mailed it to Lisa. On his way home, he would stop to buy candy and a few men's fitness magazines. Sometimes he received a small bonus for his excellent work, and he was always eager to tell Lisa to expect a bigger check.

By May, Mark had gained the emotional strength and physical stamina to say to us, "My son needs me. I'm leaving." Mark walked away from Dr. G., announcing that he was well enough to function successfully on his own. We could do nothing but stand aside and watch as he prepared to depart. Dr. G. explained that Mark's return to Atlanta would only increase his stress. He pointed out that Mark had no doctors to support him in Atlanta and reminded us that Lisa still did not believe he had a bona fide illness. She thought Houston and I were overprotective parents, coddling their only child.

We bought Mark a bus ticket to Atlanta. I helped him pack and with a choked throat, bid him farewell. I had no way to stop him. Dr. G.'s send-off was not as gentle as ours. He said, "Mark will make ten months at most before he disintegrates into another psychotic episode."

Within eleven months, rejecting medication and again using alcohol and marijuana, Mark relapsed in Atlanta. He was twenty-eight.

jail

EARLY IN THE MORNING AND at exorbitant telephone rates, we learned the news that our son was again behind bars, this time in Atlanta. Mark remembered little of what occasioned his arrest. In a psychotic rage, he had drowned his stepdaughter's kitten and verbally threatened his wife. His stepdaughter, Angela, witnessed it all. With pointed finger, she had said, "He killed my cat."

Mark denied the charges, saying, "Why would I hurt her cat? I like animals. And I wouldn't hurt my wife. She knows that. Mom, please come bail me out."

This time, I simply cried. I had no idea or strategy. He spoke nonchalantly on the telephone. He seemed to have no idea of the gravity of his situation. Mark, in his mania and psychosis, had terrorized his wife and child and made them fear further harm.

At his arraignment, Mark was so ill and so unmedicated that he was not able to understand the nature of the charges against him. Later, he told me, "When the judge talked, it sounded like gibberish. Nothing made any sense." That day in court, Mark waived all of his rights. "I didn't know what else to do," he said.

Mark wrote about his confusion:

In the padded-room of my heart,
A madman suffers.
He moves, and ants scale tender stems of my nerves.
He will not be still.
Nor will he be silent.
His screams are all that's left to fill the void that was love.
If only there was a key to release him,
he'd be free to murder pain.

One of Mark's charges was a felony crime. Houston and I knew we needed an excellent criminal lawyer. We found Dave Carson, a young litigator who was beginning a new group practice. Mark was not lucid enough even to confer with him. Dave, nevertheless, immediately petitioned the court to reduce the charges to consider Mark a first-time offender. Dave asked that Mark remain under medical supervision until he was able to have a coherent conversation with his attorney and understand the charges brought against him. The judge granted his petitions. Lisa informed us that Mark could no longer come back to their apartment. Eventually, they separated, with a divorce pending. We could only wait and hope that Mark took the medicine provided in jail. All inmates in the medical unit had a choice about whether to accept medication.

The judge set Mark's bail at $5,000 with the caveat that Mark be released to the custody of his parents or, with proof, to a supervised living facility. In either instance, there needed to be medical evaluation, followed by treatment. Mark's lawyer began immediately to search for a bondsman. He was refused at every turn because Houston and I were out-of-state residents. Georgia law is not favorable to out-of-state bond guarantors. Without bond, Mark would remain in jail.

By Mark's second week of confinement, Dave told us that Mark had been taking his medication regularly and was becoming more lucid. He arranged a meeting with Mark to discuss his case. Dave felt that every hour Mark remained inside, his chances of getting into trouble increased. Mark was not just sitting idly in his cell. He had already been relegated to solitary confinement for verbal fights. Houston and I called every day, and every day Mark was allowed to talk, he expressed anger toward one inmate or another. Someone had stolen part of his breakfast or knocked over a drink and wet his shirt. Mark was definitely feeling hemmed in. We had to get him out of jail, and we were working against time. Ultimately, Mark was sentenced with a steep fine, community service, and five years of probation. Once Mark completed probation, the court was supposed to expunge his record.

I earnestly began scouring the yellow pages for rehabilitation centers, not knowing where to find a facility that treated mental illness as well as addiction. I got referrals and hoped I could locate an appropriate place in Atlanta. We could not bring Mark home with us again, and it was imperative that he be released from jail to a facility that could treat his illness.

After days of calling and being refused by more than a few mental health agencies, I discovered rather quickly that most residential rehabilitation facilities would not accept a client who was on the drug Haldol or whose last place of residence had been jail. Haldol had the reputation of being used as a temporary treatment for the most severe cases of mental illness. I persisted with my calls. SAFE was the first suitable place I found that might accept Mark directly from jail. A telephone volunteer working for mental health placement had made the suggestion. I explained that we needed a place with calm surroundings and privileges that allowed our son some freedom for going off-site. I worried that Mark would feel confined or pressured to leave before he was officially released. SAFE required an interview. I asked if Houston and I could tour the residence and be interviewed in place of our son, who was incarcerated. The director was patient and a good listener. He agreed to our proposal as long as he could also speak with Mark by telephone. Houston and I made arrangements to fly to Atlanta.

When Mark called, we told him our plans to visit and interview at SAFE. I asked him what he wanted and needed in a residential setting. As if he had been expecting the question, he answered, "I need space to breathe. I want to be able to walk outside. I need decent food—not great, just decent. I need to be able to leave when I want to."

SAFE was placid, with new age surroundings of candles and soft music. The grounds were plush and set back from a main highway. The director was satisfied with Mark's telephone interview. SAFE would accept him from jail and would manage and distribute his medication. Mark, however, would need his own psychiatrist. Houston and I were relieved that Mark would have a place to live after jail, but we sighed under the weight of the additional expenses. The bottom line was that he would be safe. In time, we would figure out the rest.

Our next stop was Fulton County Jail to see our son. We mustered stamina for the feat. This was a first for us. At that time, Houston and I were unfamiliar with the common jail practice of frisking visitors and requiring them to remove all metal objects from their bags and pockets. Parents and loved ones behind us appeared to know the routine. They kindly pointed out the procedure to us. "This your first time?" one man asked with slight amusement. He could tell we were rookies.

Once through the machinery, we found metal folding chairs like everyone else and began our interminable wait. I had never seen so many sad and dejected faces in one place. Houston spoke to one man nearby. "How's it going?" he asked.

"I'm having a fine day," the man responded. "Bless the Lord. I just saw my brother, and now I'm waiting to see my cousin."

Then came the shout, "Baker!" Houston and I jumped to attention. We had been waiting close to two hours. The guard led us down a corridor into a cramped room. One wall was a Plexiglas window through which we could see another chair and a door. There were phone receivers on both sides. Within a few minutes, Mark entered through the other door, sat, and picked up the receiver.

"Mom . . . Dad, it's so good to see you!" he said with a broad smile. He looked rested and composed. He asked about our trip, and we exchanged small talk about the interview at SAFE. Mark was wearing a gray-blue, two-piece, wrinkled outfit with large block-print letters on the back advertising ATLANTA CORRECTIONAL FACILITY. I wanted to hold him. I could not even touch his hand.

Then I heard, through the thin walls of the cubicle next to us, a woman telling the man behind her Plexiglas partition, "Louanne sent you a message. When you see Pete, tell him she's coming next week. She couldn't come today 'cause Petey Jr.'s sick."

Were there entire family networks in this place? As lights began to flicker indicating the end of our visiting time, I put both hands onto the Plexiglas and shouted, "I love you," as if Mark could not hear. From his side of the partition, Mark touched the outline of my hands with his.

After his release, Mark remembered his time in Fulton County Jail:

My cell is stagnant and stale. I look through the steel-grated, jailhouse window at the full moon. The stark-white sphere seems to wink devilishly at me—makes me wish I could breathe fresh air. I have been cooped up too long, too many times. As tears well in my eyes (tears I dare not reveal) all I can think is that I've let everybody down I care about, including myself. I imagine myself on the surface of the moon, looking down at the earth in all its splendor. Being jailed makes me think optimistic ideals like love, beauty, and freedom are dead. Standing, still looking out through the grated window, I block out all clatter of the general population around me and wonder what it would take to shift my cosmic stars, so I could become the moon.

getting out

HOUSTON AND I RETURNED TO Philadelphia the next day. Three days later, the director of SAFE called to say, "We will accept Mark from jail, but, after one week, he will have to find another residence. We lost our funding so we have to close our doors in two weeks. I'm sorry."

Houston and I were devastated. We knew of no other facility. When Mark called, I gave him the distressing news. "Hang on, Mark," I encouraged. "I'll keep making calls. We will find something."

Luckily, I found MARR, Metro Atlanta Recovery Residences, after several phone calls. MARR's residential population suffered with drug and alcohol addiction. MARR facilitators encouraged spirituality and required patients to adhere to the twelve-step program of Alcoholics Anonymous. The staff had some experience with patients diagnosed with bipolar disorder. I immediately made the call, and Houston and I arranged another trip to Atlanta.

Our plan was tentative. We would visit MARR and also try to find a bondsman who would work with us despite the fact that we lived out of state. Once settled in our hotel in downtown Atlanta, we traveled a great distance to the area near the jail where bondsmen's offices were as numerous as bodegas. They seemed to form a township of their own. As we drove the intersecting streets, we saw occasional beggars rummaging dumpsters or slumped over paper-bagged bottles. There were only a few women and children, and there were not many whites. Each of the bail-bondsmen businesses had a clever sign advertising IT'S EASY TO GET YOUR LOVED ONE OUT OF JAIL! or WE BRING HIM TO YOU! On a sultry summer's day, we knocked on several of the closed doors only to realize we had arrived at noon, southern lunchtime.

After roaming another half hour, I saw a sign that read JET BONDING. I called to Houston from across the street, "I'll bet that one's black owned! Let's try it." We chuckled at our inside joke. The name reminded me of the black news digest *Jet*, known so well in the African American community. Surely the name on the door was meant to attract black clients.

The office was open, and inside we saw only African Americans, some waiting and others obviously working as staff. Securing bail money was new to us. We greeted everyone as if we had entered an ordinary store. Hank, the owner, was at lunch. His receptionist said, "Wait if you want to," nodding to a hard bench in the middle of the room. She never looked up from her desk. The room was sparse, with a few of the ubiquitous folding chairs. It was hot and humid, and the two air conditioning window units coughed and sputtered. Hank's receptionist took our information as other staff rustled out paper-bag lunches. The suitcase we had been lugging all day sat at our feet. It held the fresh clothes we'd brought for Mark to wear when he arrived. I hoped the new shirt and pants would fit and transform him into a presentable citizen.

Hours passed, and the air in Jet Bonding grew stuffier. This was the day Mark expected us to bail him out, and we had no way of contacting him about our delay in finding a bondsman. I began to think that the bail-bond procedure might not happen. He'll be so disappointed, I thought. Having been successfully programmed by Mark, I also thought Mark might be quite angry if we failed to get him out of jail.

Later, when I asked Mark how he felt that day, he shared this piece of writing: *Time creeps in jail. After about four weeks (or was it more?), the day of my release finally arrived. The "powers that be" decided to give me a second chance. It is a small miracle.*

On the day of release, it takes five hours for the jail to process me out. I am restless. They have somehow lost the clothes I was arrested in. I have to wear second-hand clothes out to meet my father. Nothing fits. And I've let my hair and beard grow, afraid of the possible disease from dirty, jailhouse barbershop clippers. I probably look a mess. When the last door that holds me captive finally opens, I am nervous. Will my dad be angry with me? Will he speak to me? Maybe my dad won't come. This is, after all, another time in jail. Suddenly, I am overcome with a feeling of intense embarrassment.

At three o'clock, Hank, the African American owner of Jet Bonding, came back from lunch, and office business restarted. We explained to Hank our dilemma of being out-of-state residents and needing to bail our son out of Fulton County Jail.

"He's sick. He has bipolar disorder," I explained. "We are the only ones who can bail him out. We don't know anyone in Georgia who could guarantee bond."

Hank thought for a few moments as he rifled papers, and then, as if reading from a statute, informed us that it was highly unusual for Georgia to grant out-of-state guarantors the right to pay for a Georgia inmate. From their expressions of casual interest, it was clear that Hank and his staff had heard many stories like ours. There were no cubicles to soften the lack of privacy.

Then a curious thing happened. As he examined our driver's licenses and passports, Hank began to ask Houston questions: "So, where were you born? What do you do for a living? Where did you go to college?"

Not understanding what the questions might have to do with getting bail money, Houston was frightened not to answer. He even tried to make a feeble joke about being lucky to go to college at all. Hank gave no indication he had heard and offhandedly asked, "Are you the Houston Baker who wrote *Black Literature in America*?"

This was Houston's first edited book, written in the 1970s. He hesitated and stuttered for a moment but answered, "Yes, I am."

Hank looked at him with a wry smile and said, "You know, I have that book, and I read in it a lot. I keep it on my nightstand. It has been really important to me." With a quiet voice, he asked, "Do you have $500? That's what you need for your down payment on the bond."

Houston, still startled, scrambled for our checkbook. A relaxed silence crept into the room, and the staff became decidedly friendlier. We signed papers agreeing that Jet Bonding had the right to collect the remainder of the $5,000 bond if Mark ran away. Hank added, "If he is lost, rest assured we *will* find him and return him to jail."

All we could do was keep nodding. We heard Hank call the jail and request that Mark Baker be processed out and brought over to Jet Bonding. The agency would vouch for Mark's whereabouts, he said, "until his hearing or his guaranteed return. He is being released into the custody of his out-of-state parents." With a mixture of emotions, we waited for Mark to be brought over to us from the jail.

Later, in recovery, Mark wrote about his last day inside:

It's morning. So early the sun hasn't decided to awaken. The moon has left the frame of my window, leaving a pre-dawn black canvas. Lights went out at eleven p.m. the night before. It must be about five a.m. It feels like it's only been a few hours since I fell asleep. I am angry to be awakened at such an early hour by glaring overhead lights and loud voices. It makes the day so long. But, it is breakfast time. In jail, the only thing more coveted than the hazy, dream-laden escape of sleep, is food. This morning, like every other morning, the inmates rush to stand in line on the stairs leading to the second tier. There is shoving and pushing, some arguing. But for the most part, we line up in an orderly fashion. We know that the faster we line up and shut up, the faster we will get food. To this day, I have nightmares about the thick, non-descript, brown-filled trays the guards served. Each tray had three compartments. And there was a roach in one of my compartments. Now, that's heavy. I know getting another tray is out of the question. So, I close my mind, flick off the roach, sit down, and begin eating.

It was nearly 6:00 PM when guards finally brought Mark over to Jet Bonding from jail. It was good he had eaten at least one meal that day. I did not immediately recognize our son. He had been in jail for five weeks. He had a beard below his chin, and his mustache was overgrown. The hair on his head was long and wild. He looked like one of the beggars we had passed on the street earlier that day. I had the feeling he was uncomfortable in my presence; he kept edging away from me. I was not sure if he was embarrassed, overmedicated, or feeling paranoid. The clothes he wore were not his own. The guards had been unable to find his belongings, so Mark had taken a mismatched outfit from the bin of discarded clothing. I was saddened by the way the shirt and drawstring pants hung on his frail frame. Mark moved at a snail's pace, as if his limbs were stiff. He uttered a quiet "Hi, Mom," and that was all.

Hank brusquely directed him to "get up and move over to the right. We need a picture of you."

Mark said nothing and obeyed. After the snapshot, Houston interrupted the awkwardness of the moment and asked, "Want to get cleaned up and changed? Your Mom bought you some new clothes. I'll give you a hand."

Mark nodded and followed his father. They disappeared into a restroom barely large enough for one. Houston cut Mark's hair and helped him shave and dress for the world. With hair and odd clothes bagged for trash, Mark emerged resembling the son I knew. Still, he flinched each time I came near him. When I smiled and suggested,

"Come sit next to me," he leapt to attention and did exactly what I said. He never attempted eye contact.

Hank again gestured to Mark. "Over here," he said, pointing to a stool. Mark quickly obeyed. "One more picture," Hank chuckled, "so we'll know what you look like when we have to go lookin' for you."

Mark was free, paid for, and delivered.

rehab

THE FIRST NIGHT, THE THREE of us shared a two-room unit in a downtown hotel. My nerves were on edge, and I barely slept. Mark was in our custody, and we could not lose sight of him. At first light, we went to breakfast at a local diner. We tried to practice and prepare for our MARR interview, just hours away.

"What if they won't take him?" I whispered to Houston. His silence told me that he shared the same fear. We had no other plan if MARR did not accept Mark for residential living. Mark could not sit still at the diner. He kept getting up and moving around the eating area. He said little. I asked him if he was feeling scared. He just stared back at me. When Mark was released from jail, the guards gave him discharge papers but no medication. We were all flying without parachutes.

Administrators at MARR welcomed us when we arrived. Their effusive introductions reminded me of college admissions interviewers. After a tour of the grounds, we attended meetings with doctors, counselors, and the director himself. I could feel Mark's tension. I feared he might snap at someone's question and respond inappropriately. It was clear that all eyes were on Mark. These were tests I wanted him to pass. One counselor, out of the blue, asked, "So, when did you stop using cocaine, Mark?"

Even I was startled. I held my breath during the moment's silence. Mark returned the counselor's stare and replied, "I never used coke. I only used grass."

The director smoothly brought the conversation to a close and told us there would be an administrative staff meeting to discuss Mark's case. Before we left the room, the same counselor looked back at Mark and asked again, "Mark, when did you stop using cocaine?" Mark gave the same reply.

Mark had given permission for Houston and me to stay during his interviews. We hoped this was a good sign, an indication to us that he was making a commitment to getting well. The interview intake process was extensive and grueling. We heard details about Mark's life that surprised us. During the eleven months since he left us, he had been hospitalized once already, and we had not known about it. He'd had several run-ins with the police for disorderly conduct. He regularly smoked marijuana and drank alcohol. During an interview later in the day, Mark finally admitted he had used cocaine, more than once. In the presence of strangers, we learned that our son's recent past had been a nightmare.

After hours of deliberation, administrators at MARR agreed that, while Mark was being evaluated for correctness of placement, he could live in the facility and attend daily life classes and therapeutic support groups. Since his case involved bipolar disorder, as well as addiction, he would be under close supervision. At the time, I was so relieved that Mark had a safe place to live that I did not take in the conditional nature of their decision.

At the MARR facility, Mark shared an apartment with three older men who agreed to make room for him. The apartment was clean and appropriately appointed, with just enough space. As a team, the men were responsible for cleaning, shopping, cooking, and conducting AA meetings each evening. They shared the maintenance of the four-bedroom, two-bathroom apartment and attended daily group-therapy sessions and classes devoted to finding employment. The facility would provide Mark with extra supervised care, as well as assistance with his medication.

Mark was angry, even indignant, about the rules at MARR. He wrote about his first day:

The man at the rehab center checked my suitcase when I was admitted. He took my mouthwash out and never gave it back. What the fuck? My mouthwash!?! "It has alcohol in it," was all I was told. I had no personal privacy. What a humiliation! These people actually felt that my history of drug abuse was so severe I might actually stoop so low as to drink mouthwash for a cheap high. I checked my face in the mirror for bruises 'cause I sure felt slapped in the face—and I had been socked hard. Now, I couldn't even use mouthwash!

As a newcomer, Mark was restricted to campus for two weeks. If he decided to leave the program, nobody would stop him. MARR was a voluntary program. One rule in particular was especially challenging: telephone calls were not allowed during those first weeks. Houston and I had become accustomed to talking with Mark on a regular basis, even when he was in jail. The telephone was our mutual lifeline. I could not fathom such tough love, but I also did not understand the twelve-step program for alcoholics. I had no experience with addiction and alcoholism.

During Mark's stay at MARR, we continued to study the available literature on bipolar disorder, especially the connection between bipolar disorder and addiction. We learned that people with bipolar disorder, if not diagnosed and treated, commonly use alcohol and drugs to self-medicate their illness. As a result, they become doubly afflicted. When Mark was in psychological pain, he found that using marijuana brought him comfort. He was very aware of the extent of his addiction to marijuana and alcohol.

In his notebooks, he confided:

I was a fiend who had become a fiend. A devil of a drug addict. And, still, I would have taken to the grave the fact that I knew the guys I was in rehab with were worse off than I. I was only addicted to Cannabis. What was I doing with cocaine and heroin addicts? It wasn't fair and nobody seemed to understand. I was fine. I just needed to cut back a little—you know, smoke in moderation. Then,

I could smoke marijuana with no negative consequences. And, so
what if I died drinking and doing drugs—at least I would die happy.

At the end of Mark's first day at MARR, we made our exhausted
farewells, assuring him we would stop by before leaving Atlanta. He
did not want to be left in that place. We reminded him, "It's better
than jail."

Years later, Mark confessed that during his first week at MARR,
his only thoughts had been about getting high:

> *Grass,*
> *You crash into my consciousness*
> *like sparrows into glass.*
> *I wish I could say I at least tried*
> *to free myself from your embrace,*
> *but I am a victim of complacency,*
> *guilty of no attempt at escape.*
> *Instead,*
> *I sit on psyche's prison bed*
> *And write love letters to you –*
> *Dear Mary Jane,*
> *Let us never forget the*
> *times spent erasing the pain,*
> *floating through space and*
> *periods of time . . .*
> *periods of time . . .*
> *periods of time . . .*
> *Lost as a comma*
> *in corn fields of text.*
> *Your image returns to me now*
> *in dreams of perfect strains.*

a change of plans

WE LEFT MARK AT METRO Atlanta Recovery Residences and returned home to Philadelphia. Two weeks later, the director of MARR called to inform us that Mark's case had been reviewed further; the staff of doctors and counselors had determined that Mark had been inappropriately placed in their facility. They had made great efforts to tailor the program to meet Mark's needs, but they concluded that Mark needed cognitive not confrontational therapy. His dual diagnosis meant that confrontational therapy could easily trigger a manic and violent response. Mark needed to be transferred immediately.

MARR referred our son to a place called Skyland Trail, an Atlanta mental health facility that would accept Mark despite his recent stint in jail and his dual diagnosis. The MARR director told us, "They don't have a bed right now. Maybe in a few weeks." Skyland Trail would treat Mark's bipolar disorder as well as his addiction.

"While you're waiting, why not take a family trip?" one MARR counselor suggested. He obviously had no idea what a family trip would mean for us with Mark in such a state, but he continued, "Go play some golf. In a couple of weeks, perhaps Skyland Trail will have a bed for Mark. That's the best place for him."

We did not play golf, and we were quite aware of the counselor's use of the word "perhaps."

"The wait list is short," he said, trying to put us at ease.

Once again, Mark was being released from a facility with nowhere to go. Without medication, he would eventually explode into another episode. I could feel the pressure building. When Mark heard the discouraging news about MARR and the possible shift to another facility, his agitation grew. His attempt to live drug-free was already proving to be a difficult transition for him. He wrote:

The mental trickery essential to my surviving jail almost killed me upon my release. Since once released, nothing was as I had imagined. I was as heartbroken as an earthworm in dirt void of rain. Life was as dead to me as a bloodstained flightless white dove. I had entertained a torrid love affair with Cannabisitiva that had turned at some point fatal in nature. I simply could not entertain the thought of going forever without substance—without the daily tongue kiss of Mary Jane. What would I do?

When I heard that Mark would have to leave MARR, I instantly became the imploring mother: "Please, there must be some way you can let Mark stay at MARR—another week, just a few more days, until Skyland Trail finds a bed for him. He can't come back home with us."

My pleading sent the staff and doctors back into consultation. They decided Mark could remain at MARR one additional week, absolutely no longer. Mark's history of mania and violent behavior made him a possible threat to others in the program. Houston and I anxiously waited for Skyland Trail to respond.

Fortunately, an administrator from Skyland Trail called a few days later to let us know they had space for Mark. We flew to Atlanta, checked Mark out of the MARR facility, and drove him to Skyland Trail the same day.

This time, Houston and I felt more confident going into the interview. Arriving at Skyland, we were delighted to find an over-sized but unassuming white frame house set back from busy Peachtree Boulevard. The facility was tucked into a wooded area with a small koi pond and flowers in abundance. The receptionist was welcoming and invited us to wait in the staff kitchen until our meeting with Dr. Lassiter, the clinical director.

"I apologize for the kitchen," he smiled and greeted us. "We're doing some renovations."

Dr. Lassiter was a quiet man. His interview style was easy and unhurried, and Molly, the resident cat, sauntered in during the interview. Mark found Molly's presence settling, and he stroked her throughout the conversation. The kitchen setting relaxed all of us. The manner of Skyland Trail was informal yet efficient and professional. Mark was straightforward, candidly answering all of Dr. Lassiter's questions. Mark was more relaxed than he had been during the MARR interviews a few weeks prior.

At the end of our conversation, Dr. Lassiter gave us the news that Mark was welcome at Skyland Trail. Later in the afternoon, he would be able to check in. After our extremely thorough interview and conversation, we toured the facility with Dr. Lassiter. He introduced Mark to the staff as the new Skyland Trail resident. For the moment, Mark's temporary diagnosis would be "affective disorder, otherwise unspecified." The Skyland Trail team of psychiatrists would strive for a specific diagnosis in the coming months. No time constraints were attached to Mark's stay. Dr. Lassiter assured us Mark would be safe.

As we walked around the first day, I saw a number of people with shuffling gaits and unblinking eyes. I shuddered to think that in a few weeks, Mark might look that way too. Mark wrote about his arrival at Skyland:

I was not like these people. It was like animal instinct to resist being put in a long-term mental health facility. Was I crazy?? When I first arrived, I saw people talking to themselves, pacing back and forth and acting strangely. I had a long time ago bought into the societal, Hollywood image of the mentally ill so I was prejudiced going in. They were all freaks as far as I was concerned. I was convinced, just like I was convinced I was not a real drug addict, that I was NOT mentally ill, that I was nothing like these people!

One of the counselors offered to show us the apartment Mark would share with another man, James, an older, longtime resident of Skyland Trail. "We try to match apartment mates closer in age," she explained. "But this is the only bed we have available."

The apartment was amply spacious, with a bedroom on each side of a narrow hallway, a shared bathroom, and a common living room and kitchen. James and Mark were responsible for the maintenance of their shared spaces, and each was responsible for maintaining his own bedroom. Skyland residents took their meals in a common dining area in the main building, so James and Mark would only need the kitchen for snacks, cold drinks, and coffee. Mark would have his turn at team dinner preparation since everyone eventually planned and helped to serve the evening meal. We were pleased that Mark would become responsible for others, as well as himself.

While Houston provided final details for the Skyland staff, I helped Mark unpack his belongings. I tried to stay upbeat. I chatted nonstop about how beautiful the surroundings were and reminded him about the many opportunities for playing basketball, painting, and meeting new people. "You can even write poetry by the koi pond," I suggested.

I knew I had to keep talking. The alternative was crying. For some odd reason, I felt horribly sad. I knew Mark needed to be in a place like Skyland Trail, but I did not want to leave him. His two weeks at MARR had evened out his disposition. His psychiatric medication, Depakote, was working well. His mood was soft and caring. During the months Mark had been in and out of jail and hospitals, he had lost the easy smiles and quick humor of his youth. I missed them. I had almost forgotten the gentle, sensitive Mark. Now, for a brief moment, he had come back to me.

While we were enjoying small talk, Mark's new roommate, James, came into the apartment. He looked at us quizzically but never spoke. He was about fifty, and he suffered from schizophrenia. We introduced ourselves, but James said nothing. He contorted his face, mumbled a few incomprehensible words, and disappeared into the back of the apartment. Mark and I looked at each other, wondering if James was pleased or upset at Mark's presence. Suddenly, we felt we should whisper. Houston returned and felt the awkwardness.

"So, what just happened here?" he asked.

"Just getting Mark set up," I said. We only mentioned that James had come home and was resting. Houston and I gathered our belongings to depart Skyland Trail, and I tried to delay leaving.

"Shouldn't we talk to somebody about dispensing medicine for Mark?" I asked.

"Mark really is OK," Houston assured me, gently rubbing my back. "They have all the information they need."

Mark sidled up to me and whispered, "Mom, I cannot stay here. Don't leave me here." Little did he know how much I empathized with him. I hugged him tightly but did not let myself waver.

"It won't be for long, sweetheart. We will be back soon. They're going to make you well here," I said.

I bit hard on the inside of my lip to hold back the tears. Once we turned out of the parking lot, I began to sob at full volume. I cried all the way to the airport.

Mark stayed in residence at Skyland Trail for almost one year. We talked at least three times a week by telephone. On our first visit back to Skyland about a month later, he eagerly told us of Lydia, his newest friend. They met on a group field trip, and she was hoping to meet us during the visit. Contrary to Mark's story that he did not know many people, he seemed very much a part of the community.

When we visited again, months later, he seemed more stable, and he appeared to be fully integrated into his life at Skyland. He did not even protest the routine of the days. By telephone, he told us that he liked his therapist, who thought he was making progress. Mark's writing recalls his feelings during this period:

I was still very reluctant about the whole, "admitting I was mentally ill and would be for the rest of my life" thing. I didn't think there was anyone in the world like me. I felt that my plight and predicament were unique. I now realize how narcissistic my thinking was. At no time was this narcissism more evident than when I first entered a residential mental health center for long-term treatment. There were patients my age at the center who were surviving with bipolar disorder. For the first time, I met others who were experiencing a similar hell. Those patients in my age group and at the same place in their recovery as I made bipolar illness never again seem lonely. Over cigarettes, we would sit on the porch and discuss what had brought us to that place. I saw others taking medication for their ailments. So, it was around this same time that I began willingly taking my own medication. As the thick fog of insanity slowly began to lift, I began to come to terms with the relieving fact that no one was out to get me—that I was mentally ill, but given time, faith, patience, and caring loved ones, I would eventually be all right. I was not alone and so I was, for the first time in ages, it seemed, somewhat happy.

Houston and I were startled when Mark began asking, "How much longer do I have to stay in here?" He had been in residence six months. He began to complain about the food and about James's habit of talking to himself late at night. "I can hear him through the walls," Mark told us. His comfort seemed to vanish almost as quickly as it had come. We thought he was resigned to staying at Skyland for treatment, but Mark began to urge us to let him move on.

The next stage of recovery and rehabilitation for Mark was to move into off-campus independent living. This usually occurred after at least one year in communal residence. Mark's medication seemed balanced, but his therapist was somewhat reluctant to approve such a dramatic change so early. The apartment complex was half a block from the main offices of Skyland Trail. Mark would have no problem getting to day-treatment sessions. He made it clear that he was ready. After nine months of communal residential living, Mark had become a poster boy for Skyland: "a Skyland Trail success story," his fellow clients teasingly called him. He had a part-time job off campus, working for a mental health peer project connected to Emory. He was paying his own bills, keeping a clean, neat apartment (in spite of James), participating in and leading AA dual diagnosis groups, and regularly meeting with his therapist, who reported steady improvement.

Mark became fluent in the language of recovery. He understood the meaning of compliance and relapse, his need for a twelve-step program, and the necessity of regular medication for his bipolar disorder. He had even helped to start the dual diagnosis support group at Skyland. He was a model resident. Best of all, he was writing again.

trying independence

MARK PUSHED HARD TO BE approved for off-campus independent living. He let everyone know that he was beginning to repeat
the content material of his "life courses." There was no room for
growth, he contended. He was fed up and told me, "Boredom is
stressful too, you know." Mark convinced us and his therapists that
he could negotiate living alone and that it would be less distracting
than having a housemate. Recalling the difficulties he had been having with James, we understood. Mark would continue his therapy
and day-treatment classes at the main facility. He would be expected
at the facility for dinner, and his medication would remain in the
office. The plan seemed feasible, and it would give Mark a sense
of growth and progress. During Mark's tenth month, the Skyland
clinical team recommended Mark for independent living.

Houston and I helped Mark move into his new space. As we
cleaned, hung curtains, and mopped floors, we remembered the
fun we had had moving him into his graduate student apartment
in Los Angeles. We played music and sang much too loudly as we
prepared one more apartment for Mark's occupancy. Houston and
I felt positive about Mark's single living arrangement. We told ourselves that bipolar episodes and drug relapses were things of the
past. We believed in Mark's dedication to recovery.

Skyland Trail also believed in his dedication. The director asked
Mark to participate in a Skyland promotional video for prospective
clients and their families. By appearing in the video, Mark would
disclose his mental illness. I, however, was not sure I was ready for
this public disclosure. But I swallowed my own lack of bravery and
praised Mark for his courage.

In the promotional video, Mark describes how Skyland Trail "saved me from the streets" and provided a path to recovery. To this day, whenever I watch this video, I find it extremely moving. When I see how Mark looks onscreen, overweight from his medication, writing checks to pay bills in his squeaky-clean apartment, I am amazed at how far he traveled. There was a time when Mark used check-cashing storefronts as his bank and never, ever paid his bills. He readily admits, on camera, that this is the first time in years he has been able to sit long enough in one place to finish paying all of his bills. As the camera pans across the room, I glimpse the table and chairs for two and remember when Houston and I bought the set for him in a small shop in Atlanta. I can see a portion of the denim-blue sleep sofa that used to live in the den of our Philadelphia home. Leaving Mark in his new apartment was so much easier than leaving him the first time for admission to the Skyland Trail communal residence.

Mark's living arrangement suited him well. He lived only a short distance from the main building of Skyland and was able to get to his classes and therapy sessions on time. Shortly after settling in, Mark accepted a part-time, unpaid job writing short articles on mental illness for a local hospital connected with Skyland Trail's client recovery program. Mark's task was to write for their peer newsletter, which provided mentorship for newer, less seasoned mental health consumers. Mark loved writing articles for the newsletter. His editor accepted one of his pieces, "The Road Less Traveled" as a lead contribution. In it, Mark encouraged communication: "There is a certain relief in knowing that you are not the sole survivor of the storm. When things clear, it is comforting to see others trying to find their way—lost but alive." Houston and I were extremely proud of Mark's efforts. We were also relieved that he was safe, acclimating to his new surroundings, and working on a project.

A few months later, after telling us that he and Lisa were barely communicating, Mark mentioned divorce. Months before, Lisa had told Mark that she did not want him to return to their apartment. He felt sure they would never resume their life together. We suggested that Mark speak with his criminal defense lawyer to get a referral for a divorce attorney. We wondered whether a legal separation, not a divorce, would be the easier, less expensive route to take.

Since Mark was still undergoing treatment at Skyland, Houston and I agreed to meet with the divorce lawyer in his place. Neither of us knew what to expect. Mr. Harrison was straightforward but kind: "You know what the worst part of this process is going to be? Placing their son in the right home," he said, answering his own question. "Will they fight over the child?" he asked.

We assured him that Lisa and Mark wanted the best for their son. Jack, now two and a half, was a priority for both of them. Then the lawyer told us the cost of divorce: "$2,000 is the retainer. The cost will be about $6,000. Of course you'll also need funds along the way for incidentals, like payment for court documents and a guardian *ad litem*." I am sure he heard my sharp intake of breath. "It doesn't seem to me that Lisa or Mark is in a position to pay. Is that correct?" he asked.

Houston and I exchanged glances. The amounts were steep. We thanked Mr. Harrison for his time and patience. He gave us his card, saying we could always contact him at a later time if we wished to pursue the divorce. At the hotel later, Houston and I sat down to figure out what we could afford. We were already sending money regularly to Lisa for Jack's care in Atlanta. Shortly, Mark would be released from Skyland altogether and presumably would need help to pay his rent. Our own salaries were stretching out to three households. We loved our son, who had no job and no promise of one. We loved our grandson, Jack. But at this point, we could not take on the additional burden of paying for a divorce.

We called Mark to give him the news that he and Lisa could not divorce without hiring a lawyer. Only the court could determine the legal custody of Jack, a minor. "Lisa and I can split the responsibility," said Mark. "We would both take care of him. We both want the divorce. I mean, you can get a divorce online. We don't own anything," explained Mark.

"That would make it easy," I answered, "but the law states that when a child is involved, the court decides the best home for the child. Your father and I have talked. The cost of a divorce is too much for us, given all the other expenses we are already covering. We can't do it."

Houston and I called Attorney Harrison and told him that Mark could not continue with divorce proceedings at this time. It would be up to Mark to contact him at a later date. Meanwhile, Mark and Lisa remained separated. Jack lived with his mother while Mark completed his treatment in independent care at Skyland.

On the home front, Lisa, her daughter, and Jack lived in an apartment building not far from Lisa's Aunt Willa. Willa was especially close to the children. Mark told me that Jack went to a neighborhood daycare center each day, along with his sister. Lisa worked in the fast-food industry, and her hours changed weekly. I could never keep up with Lisa's job schedule. Some days, she worked 9:00 AM to closing, and other days she worked the night shift. If Lisa was displeased with the work conditions, she quit and looked for a job in another restaurant. Her main concern was making enough money to keep her children with her. Lisa told me she could always count on Willa to watch the children at a moment's notice. Both children adored their Aunt Willa.

Because Mark and Lisa were no longer a couple, I did not feel I could call Lisa's apartment whenever I pleased. I allowed myself one phone call per week. If Lisa was out, I left a message inquiring about Jack on her answering machine. She, in turn, would call back to say Jack was fine. My relationship with Lisa was comprised mostly of phone messages. Whenever Jack was with Willa, Willa called, and Houston and I got to speak with our grandson. We never figured out how to negotiate the delicate situation in Atlanta. I missed hearing Jack's voice. We painfully accepted that we were grandparents in absentia. We never forgot special holidays or Jack's birthday, and whenever we went to Atlanta to see Mark, we arranged, through Willa, to see Jack. At least, periodically, he saw our faces, and we got to give him hugs and kisses. I always felt that Jack knew how much we loved him.

One evening, Willa called unexpectedly. I could hear the distress in her voice: "Lisa and I had an argument. I finally called her 'cause I had not seen the children in a few weeks. I was missing them. An operator message said the number had been changed. I went to the house, and no one answered the door. I'm really worried. I asked around, and nobody has seen Lisa or the children! What should I do?"

Houston and I were upset by this news. We had not heard from Lisa in a while either. We suggested that Willa call the police right away since she seemed terribly disconcerted. Willa was adamant about not involving police, however, because "they could do something, like take the children away." We just listened. Obviously, Willa knew more about Lisa and her situation than we did.

Eventually, Willa called back to say, "I found Lisa. She's staying with a friend for a while. I don't know any more right now."

A day later, Willa called to say she had located Jack. Lisa had left Jack with the parents of another friend.

"Don't worry," Willa assured us. "I'm on my way to get Jack right now. He'll stay with me. He'll be just fine." The relief in her voice calmed me.

With both Mark and Lisa in difficult situations, Houston and I had to give serious consideration to Jack's care and guardianship. Jack was virtually parentless. His father was under psychiatric care, and his mother was missing somewhere in Atlanta. We had no further details. Mark wanted to be an active parent, but he was still in treatment at Skyland and also on probation in the state of Georgia. We wanted to help Mark, and we also wanted Jack to be near both his parents in Atlanta.

Houston and I immediately knew we needed to help Mark and Lisa get a divorce. Doing nothing was no longer possible. Houston and I decided to borrow against our retirement account in order to cover the cost. The next day, I called the divorce attorney, Mr. Harrison, and told him we wanted to reopen Mark's divorce case. I explained the new situation and our concerns for Jack. We understood what the divorce proceedings would cost us, but Lisa's unexplained disappearance was a wake-up call.

Attorney Harrison informed us that as long as Mark was on probation, Mark would have to share the custody of Jack with another adult. His advice: "Since you want Jack to stay in Atlanta near his parents, what about Lisa's aunt? Does Jack have a good relationship with her? If so, perhaps she would be willing to accept temporary custody of Jack until Mark is released from Skyland and has satisfied his probation requirements."

Excited by this possibility, I telephoned Willa immediately and told her the lawyer's suggestion. Willa, the only one in contact with Lisa, called us a few days later to say that she and Lisa had decided to petition the court on Jack's behalf and have Willa act as temporary guardian.

The court granted Mark and Lisa a divorce. They gave Jack's temporary legal guardianship to Willa and granted Mark parental rights of visitation. Houston and I assured Willa that, in addition to the stipend she would receive from the court, we would provide financial support for Jack. Willa was pleased and responded, "I know we will all be OK. Mark and I work really good together. I love Jack, and he knows my family."

Houston and I knew that Willa would take excellent care of Jack. We hoped the court-sanctioned arrangement would provide the best, and least disruptive, situation for Jack.

In November of that year, we invited Mark to come home for Thanksgiving. Houston and I had accepted new teaching positions and had just moved to North Carolina. Thinking Mark would be lonely without his family, we offered to send him a plane ticket to fly to Durham. When he called back, he said, "Thanks, Mom, but I think I'll stay here and have Thanksgiving with my friends."

We were delighted that Mark was making friends in his new Skyland Trail apartment complex, and he sounded so grounded. We were disappointed that we would not see him during the holiday. Also, we were a little worried. Secretly, I wondered if he was trying to distance himself or to hide. I was afraid that such hiding might be a cover for impending illness.

I concealed my qualms and said, "Fine. We will miss you. We'll see you at Christmas!"

wrecked yuletide

THE WEEKS BETWEEN THANKSGIVING AND Christmas seemed extremely short that year. We spoke to Mark several times, but our conversations were unremarkable. When we called to ask Mark when he would arrive for Christmas, he announced again, "I think I'll stay here with my friends." My Thanksgiving worries resurfaced. Mark told me that his Skyland classes were better than ever and that, according to his therapist, he was progressing in his treatment. But as Mark talked, his tone became increasingly defensive and edgy. I knew I needed to be careful with my words. The Pollyanna in me prayed, *Let me be wrong this time.*

Once off the telephone, Houston and I agreed that Mark was not himself. We looked at each other, wondering if we had made the right decision to support Mark's move into independent living. Was our son on the brink of another episode? Since relocating to North Carolina, we had become accustomed to hurricane warnings. We thought of this latest warning sign from Mark in Atlanta, his edginess, as a threat of impending rough weather. If Mark descended back into bipolar mania, Houston and I would be limited in our ability to help him. We had no power of attorney or power of medical attorney. Our hands were tied. If Mark refused treatment, his illness would once again take over his life.

We made emergency calls asking for advice from Mark's lawyer, his therapist in Atlanta, and even his former doctors in Philadelphia. Mark's lawyer advised, "Whatever you do, do not come to Atlanta. This is Mark's city. You don't know what you'll find here. Sit tight, and trust me. There is nothing more you can do right now.

You'll just make trouble for yourselves." Until there was something to react to, we could only wait.

On December 18, Mark's birthday, Houston and I revisited this wisdom. Without knowing Mark's situation, there could be no Christmas for us. We decided to drive to Atlanta and called Mark to let him know. In the brightest phone voice I could muster, I said, "Mark, guess what? Since you can't get to us for Christmas, your father and I decided to come to you! How does that sound?"

After a slight hesitation, he said, "Really? That would be great!" Houston and I packed lightly and set a time for departure.

Around 9:00 PM two days before Christmas, we reached Mark's neighborhood. I dialed Mark's number on my cell phone to let him know we were near.

"Hey, it's Mom! How would you like to go out to dinner this evening?" A pause, but no words. "We're in your city," I continued. "We'd love to take you out to dinner."

Finally, Mark responded, "Great! I'll be ready. Just blow the horn and meet me outside." There was no invitation to come inside.

When we arrived at Mark's apartment, his bedroom lights were blazing. Music was blasting. It was December with a decided chill in the air, but his windows were wide open. There were no blinds or curtains. Where were the window coverings I had bought, carefully ironed, and hung at his windows a few months ago when he moved in? Seeing Mark's brightly lit, raucously noisy apartment in the midst of evening quiet made me wonder if neighbors had already called the police. We tapped lightly on the horn, as Mark had requested. No response. I called him again from my cell phone, and Mark said, "I hear you! I'm coming."

We waited a half hour in silence. I ventured to the front door to ring the bell. Mark's head popped out of the second-story window, and he yelled into the night, "Who's there?"

"It's your mother," I answered softly.

"I told you I'm coming!" he shouted back.

I returned to the car, warning Houston, "Be ready. He doesn't look like himself at all. He's . . . different."

When Mark showed up at the car, the three of us hugged. Houston and I wished Mark a happy birthday. In just three months, Mark had lost about seventy pounds. His mustache and short beard were gone, and his face was shaved completely clean. He was no longer wearing glasses. In place of his usually bald head was a mass of dark, shoulder-length, heavily moussed hair. Mark had been voluntarily bald for so many years that the new look startled me.

We piled into the car and searched for a place to eat. Once settled into a booth at the restaurant, Mark initiated nervous small talk. Houston and I had a hard time following his stories. He told us of a friend who could not seem to find Mark's apartment although Mark had given him several different sets of directions. He described conversations he had overheard in a grocery store. He never inquired about our impromptu trip to Atlanta. He just accepted that we were there. When we tried to enter into Mark's dialogue and ask simple questions, he accused us of not listening. His agitation mounted, and his voice grew louder.

"What's wrong with you? Don't you understand what I'm saying?"

Mark was ready for a blowup, perhaps even trying to instigate one. When his food arrived, he ate nothing. We called it an evening and offered to pick him up the next morning for a late breakfast. He accepted. I was quietly hoping to have the chance to talk with him about seeing a doctor. His behavior had once again become strange and estranging.

The next morning, Mark was dressed and ready to go when we arrived at his apartment. We ventured out for breakfast but could only find Starbucks open. Mark ordered a donut with coffee and promptly turned the sugar dispenser upside down over the cup when it arrived. He was restless and silent. We decided to take a drive and then stop at a drugstore for a few items I had forgotten to pack. As we approached the drugstore, I playfully offered Mark a "supershop." This was a treasured family game when Mark was in high school. I would stop at a store and, on the spur of the moment, declare a supershop, during which time he could select (and I would buy) anything he wanted or needed in the drugstore within a price range and a certain amount of time. I thought this might lighten the mood and even make Mark chuckle at the memory.

Mark picked up a few items but obviously did not want to play the game. I watched him deliberately wreck stacks of T-shirts and toss them back on random shelves. When I asked if he needed shaving cream, he snapped, "So what if I do?" Mark started casting sidelong stares at me, and I grew uncomfortable. I finished my shopping and headed for the cashier. Hoping he would follow, I quickly paid for our purchases and left the store.

Once back in the car, I whispered to Houston, "It didn't go well inside. Just drive."

Houston drove to kill time, a kind of wandering, meandering, sightseeing ride. Gently, as unobtrusively as possible, I asked Mark about his therapist and about his classes at Skyland. He did not respond to me directly, but I could hear him mumbling in the backseat. His mumbling sounded hostile, but I could not decipher the words. Then, in cadence with his mumbling, he began to kick the backs of our seats. Houston kept driving.

I kept talking. "Mark, we came to Atlanta because we thought you needed help. On the telephone, it sounded like you were having difficulty with your medicine. We thought we could help you, perhaps go with you to the doctor," I explained. "Is that right or wrong?"

When he did not answer, I turned around to face him and showed him the bottle of Depakote I had brought with me just in case he had run out of medicine. Our doctor in Durham had given me a few pills with instructions to dispense only if Mark was in urgent need.

It was clearly a wrong move on my part. In one swift motion, Mark ripped the bottle from my hands, opened it, put it to his mouth, and tossed back his head, swallowing multiple pills.

"You want me to take medicine?" he shouted. "There! I took your medicine. Is that what you wanted? Happy now?"

I gasped, and Houston swerved the car. From the front seat, I grabbed for the medicine bottle, and, for an instant, a smiling Mark played tug-of-war, knowing he had frightened me. I had no way of knowing how many pills he had swallowed. What if he had taken too many and had a negative reaction? What if I had put my son's life in jeopardy? Mark's energy only increased. As he drove, Houston tried unsuccessfully to talk above Mark's shouting. Mark accused his father of betraying him. He accused me of trying to dope him up with more medicine.

"Don't you believe me when I say I'm taking my medicine?" he screamed in desperation. "I'm a man. You can't make me do anything I don't want to do!"

He began to pull at Houston's arm, taunting him with physical jabs as Houston tried to drive. I had never seen Mark so out of control.

We were nearing the hotel where we were staying, so Houston pulled over to the curb. He said slowly, "Look, Mark, we cannot, we will not—"

Before Houston could finish his sentence, Mark leapt from the back seat into the driver's seat. In an instant, he had his father by the throat, pinned against the driver's seat window in a chokehold.

"Who's the smartest now?" he yelled. "Who? Who?"

His strength was massive. Houston was pinned, gasping. I reached over toward Mark, thinking I could calm him with a touch.

He swatted me like a fly. Barely audible, Houston said, "Charlotte, get out. We need to call for help."

I scrambled out of the front seat, grabbing my cell phone from the cup holder. As I stood on the side of the road, my cell phone rang, startling me. It was my brother.

"Hi. Just checking in," he said. And then he asked, "Hey, what's wrong? What's all that noise?"

My brother had no idea we were in Atlanta, and, to this day, I cannot account for his calling at precisely that moment. His timing could not have been more perfect. The ringing telephone distracted Mark from the stranglehold he had on Houston. Mark jumped out of the car and shouted at me, "Well, are you satisfied now? Did you call the police? Did you? Are they coming? I can't believe you did that! My own mother."

Every part of my body shuddered. Houston was pale, completely submissive. He spoke softly to me through the open window: "Get in the car. We have to leave this place."

I promptly got in and locked my door. Mark continued to prance around the car, shouting, "So, you're just leaving me? You're leaving me with nothing? I'm your son!"

Houston called to Mark to come closer and rolled down the window just far enough to empty his wallet into Mark's hands. He said, "Take this and get yourself home, Mark. Don't let the police find you here. We're leaving."

Mark grabbed the money but never stopped screaming and running alongside our moving car. "So, you're just going to leave me here on the street? Look at me! I have nothing! I can't believe you'd do this!"

Houston and I drove away. The police were not on their way. I had never made the call.

The next morning, after a fitful last night in Atlanta, we went to Christmas Mass at the cathedral near the hotel. I felt empty in the midst of the spirited holiday service. I glanced at Houston as the congregation began to sing. His face was wet as he bellowed out holiday carols. Mark's lawyer had been correct. We were not prepared for what we encountered in Atlanta. With the car already packed, we headed back to North Carolina.

In the days following Christmas, I thought about Mark's bizarre, abusive behavior in Atlanta. Were his actions due to unmedicated bipolar disorder? Or had he resumed using cocaine and marijuana? Earlier, we had learned that Mark had bipolar disorder along with a drug and alcohol addiction, a dual diagnosis. I never fully understood where one illness ended and the other began.

After our painful visit, Houston and I knew we needed to rethink some of our previous decisions. As the new year dawned, we decided to repossess the Toyota we had let Mark use. It was my car. I had loaned it to him so he could get to work and to his therapy appointments. During the short time we had been in Atlanta, I had looked inside the car. It was filthy, stuffed with junk and old food cartons and wrappers. The outside was crusted with dirt, and one fender was smashed in. We grew concerned that Mark, in his present state, might crash the car or hurt a pedestrian. Too tired to make yet another trip to Atlanta, we engaged a private investigator to repossess the car and return it to our home in Durham. I had no idea such a maneuver was possible.

The next day, when Mark discovered the car missing, he called us shouting into the phone, "Someone stole my car! Can you believe that? Can you believe that shit? What son of a bitch would do something like that?"

I remained silent while I thought about how I should respond. Mark was clearly enraged. When I explained to Mark that his father and I had repossessed the car because we were afraid he might crash it, he shouted a string of curses and slammed down the phone. I remember standing with the telephone in my hand, quietly shaking.

Mark writes about this period of his life:

The street vendors here do not sell soft pretzels.
They trade toxic pebbles for pocket change
until there is just lint left,
and prayers for death
on scraped knees
while pleasing the bereft.
Growing up I dreamt of finding this place
where from every corner smirks the devil's face
and people harbor hate,
nine millimeter mentalities
ruling lowly days
hoping life fades in quick, merciful ways.
Killed by unexpected strays.
Sinking in soft serenity of a fatal hit.
Remembered through surviving Polaroids.

I longed to feel the void
left by love, poverty, and hard drugs,
suspicious of friends' fond hugs,
chronic paranoia and mistrust
makes those who care miss us.
No money for birthdays, groceries, or Christmas,
this was the path I chose.
Deep woods' unwelcoming savages inviting me in,
possessed and made me one of them.
So many sins,
Then madness begins.
MIA from sanity, God and kin,
afternoons squandered
smoking shit weed, drinking gin.
Mental patients' telepathy

Raping my thoughts again
from within institutions' distant gates
not realizing my own mental state,
full of surreal realms.
A paying passenger in trains
without conductors at the helm.
Time sped oblivious ahead.
I stripped silk sheets off a tattered mattress,
now it's in this dirty bed
I am forced to lay my head.

jail again

I DECIDED TO TRY ONE more time to rescue our distressed son. Without knowing what to expect, I called Mark's probation officer in Atlanta. I recalled her name from an earlier exchange with Mark and was surprised to reach her on my first try. I started right in as soon as she identified herself.

"I am Mark Baker's mother. I know you are his probation officer because he has talked about you. I know I'm probably not supposed to call you, but I'm really scared. I don't know what else to do. I need your help."

When I paused and she did not speak, I continued. "I just saw Mark in Atlanta. I think he is off his medication. I think he is dangerous to himself and others. Please, can you help me?"

The silence was so long, I was afraid she had hung up. Then she said, "Thank you. I'm going to see your son soon. He has a scheduled visit. He is supposed to report here. I will get back to you." I heard the click of the receiver. She did not say good-bye. She never used my name or Mark's.

Within the week, shortly after Mark called again to rant with indignation about our repossessing "his car," the probation officer called me back. She told me Mark was safe. He had been arrested. When Mark arrived at her office, she had suspected he was high on illegal substances, so she called the police. Mark tested positive for street drugs and went to jail for violating the terms of his probation.

My heart ached. Our son was in jail, again. On that day, I looked in the mirror and admitted to myself that my beautiful, loving, talented son was a junkie with bipolar disorder. On the telephone, the probation officer told me she had felt sorry for Mark at the moment of his arrest. "He was very agitated. He couldn't sit still. So I rode downtown with him in the police cruiser. He seemed so fragile." I was extremely moved by her kindness. I was relieved he had not been alone.

Many years after this incident, Mark wrote about what had occurred:

It was soon time for me to make my monthly report to my probation officer. (I was on probation since I drowned my stepdaughter's kitten.) I went to the club the night before to relax and get my mind off of my impending visit. I ran into a friend, and we proceeded to get high. Somehow I made it to the probation office on time the next morning. I just knew I was going to pull off this "straight and narrow" charade. Just a five-minute session with my officer, and then I'd be released to my disheveled world again. I had not seen my psychiatrist in two months, not since he requested I take a drug test in his office, and I refused. My officer asked me if I'd been seeing my doctor; I forget what I answered. She told me to wait in the lobby while she made a call. When I reentered my probation officer's office, she had me arrested on the spot for noncompliance to the terms of my probation. It's a good thing I had no cat or dog to feed. They didn't even let me go home.

While Mark was in jail, Houston traveled alone to Atlanta to pay Mark's back rent, settle damages with the rental agency, and clear out Mark's abruptly vacated space. When he arrived at Mark's apartment, Houston called me in dismay. "My God, Charlotte, you would not believe what I'm looking at! This place is trashed!"

He knew Mark had done it. The front door was ajar, and the lock was broken. Cigarette burns covered the beige carpet, and piles of dirty clothes littered the landscape. Mark had smashed holes in closet doors and carved words into furniture. The refrigerator door hung open, displaying shelves of spoiled food. Houston said the smell in the apartment had gagged him. Magic Marker scribbles dotted the walls, and Mark had defaced his own poetry notebooks. Houston said to me, simply, "He must have been so sick." On the phone, we cried together.

I arrived the next day and joined Houston in cleaning and fixing up the apartment for the landlord's inspection. Houston had already heaved eight bags of garbage, broken dishes, and torn papers into the dumpster. He had found remnants of cigarettes and marijuana joints under the edges of the carpet and flushed them before I arrived. Together, we spent two more backbreaking days scrubbing walls and floors and hauling broken furniture to the trash heap. Whatever we did not throw away, we put into storage. There were carved letters and drawings etched into the beautiful vintage desk we had bought. There were burns on solid oak tables. There were split lampshades. Looking at the deliberate damage throughout the apartment, I forgot Mark's illness. As I scrubbed, I forgot to understand Mark's behavior as a symptom of his bipolar illness and addiction. I seethed with anger at my careless, irresponsible, selfish son. I swept the filthy carpet and sprayed Lysol to kill the odor of tobacco and marijuana.

The people at the rental agency were actually kind to us. They were neither perplexed nor aggravated about the extensive damage. They obviously knew Mark's connection to Skyland Trail. More than anything, they seemed to feel sorry for us. We paid the back rent and the fee for not leaving the apartment in spotless condition. We could do nothing about the smashed doors, ripped carpet, and writing on the walls. They did not charge us further.

While in jail, Mark called us collect every other day at the jailhouse rate of $1.25 a minute. Always eager to hear his voice, we never refused to accept the calls. Sometimes Mark said very little, until a recorded voice on the other end told us that our call would end "in approximately three minutes." I held on to the hope that if I accepted his calls, Mark would do his best to stay alive. He recounts this time in his own writing:

When arrested, I was lost in a fog of insanity. (Once during my first week in jail, I even thought my cellblock was a boat sailing in water and my fellow inmates were really my shipmates!) I was so far gone, I didn't even consider smoking or snorting coke. I was at some subconscious level relieved that I had a respite from the abuse I'd been heaping on my mind and body. Only when the fog began to lift and I firmly grasped the truth of being incarcerated—did panic set in. I did not panic because I could no longer self-medicate. I panicked because I was locked up and had no idea when I might be released. I just knew that there was a hole in my soul. I was desperate. I was frantic. And I was scared.

In the beginning, Mark's calls from jail were straightforward and pitiable, "Mom, I want to get out of here. They're treating me bad in here. The food is *awful!*"

He seemed to hear me when I said, "Not yet, Mark. You need more time to get yourself together before you get out."

On several occasions, Mark cried over the loss of contact with his son, Jack, wondering where he was and if Jack would ever understand what had happened. Mark continued to write:

My son is my heart. When it comes to Jack, I feel the self-inflicted wound of irresponsibility. One day not so long ago when we were out driving together and seeing each other regularly, I happened to glance over to find Jack looking at me with an expression that was beyond description. It was a look of respect mixed with love and awe, and it threw me when I saw it. It was as if he was saying, "You are special. I am proud to have you as my father." The fact that I hit bottom again despite the love and respect of my son, proves the cunning, baffling and powerful nature of both bipolar and drug addiction. I have asked myself countless times, "How could you do this? How could you ever let yourself slip again?!?"

After three weeks in jail, the tone of Mark's phone calls changed. "Just bail me out of here," he snapped one day. "You have the money. I know you do! Get me out!" He was angry; his voice was laced with sarcasm. With acute accuracy, Mark aimed his rage at Houston. As always, Houston steeled himself against the tirade.

Later, Mark told me, "When I hung up the phone that time, I remember I was feeling guilty. There was no reason to show my frustration to Dad. After all, he was not the reason I was incarcerated. I knew there was no bail money this time. I had no one to blame for my fall but myself. At the time, I think I was still too sick to realize that. I knew if you and Dad had refused my collect calls or failed to remind me to take things one day at a time, I could have very easily, in jail, lost my mind."

This time, Houston and I had decided that no matter what, we would not arrange for Mark's release until the lawyer called and advised us to do so.

While in jail, Mark detoxified from all the drugs and alcohol in his system. He had been incarcerated for about two months when we finally bailed him out. Houston and I insisted that Mark return to Skyland Trail for additional rehabilitation. The facility had expanded to include a new residence, Skyland South, as well as a treatment and recreational wing called the George West Health and Education Center. In the new residential building, Mark had a bright single room already furnished with a bed, dresser, and night table. The rules and regulations remained strict: no visitors in the first two weeks and no off-campus privileges. The group living and eating arrangements were the same.

Initially, Mark balked at the restrictions, but he fell into step fairly quickly. He remembered destroying his apartment. He remembered selling his new Sony computer, a gift from his uncle, for drugs. He understood why he was back in treatment. As luck would have it this time, most of the clients in the Skyland residence were close to Mark in age. I think he began, finally, to make real friends within the Skyland Trail community. When the dinner fare was not to their liking, the clients in residence pooled their change and ordered pizza. When they were given off-campus privileges, they walked as a group down to the corner store to buy toiletries and cigarettes.

As Mark became stronger, he began to write poetry and more prose. He wrote about the months prior to his arrest:

I began smoking grass again. I told my girlfriend at the time that I was planning on smoking in moderation and only at the apartment. I tricked myself into thinking it was too dangerous to drink, smoke weed, and take my psychiatric medication. Something had to be stopped. The obligatory thing for me to do, I felt at the time, was to stop taking my medication. Ironically, I was working at a job where I facilitated a peer-to-peer recovery group for people with substance abuse issues and mental illness. My co-workers began to make comments about my sagging clothes. "You need to tell your parents to give you some money for some new clothes," they would joke. Sometimes, I went to work having had no bath and no sleep at all. I'm sure there were times when I reeked of alcohol. Life was becoming unmanageable. Even though she was doing a harder drug than I, my girlfriend seemed to be able to hold it together a little better than I could. Soon, my curiosity at seeing her take bumps of powder cocaine into her nose from a door key or the corner of a playing card took over. I decided to live the high life and say, "Fuck it!" So when my girlfriend would leave her stash of powder behind and exit the room, I would quickly grab a taste, sticking a wet finger into the powder and touching it to my tongue. I soon began doing lines of powder by myself. I knew if she ever found out, we would have an argument. She said she cared about my mental illness. (In hindsight, how ridiculous does that sound?) I was at a point of no return with my addictions. I was smoking weed every day and doing powder cocaine about three times a week. I would drink now and then. I had what I like to call psychological vertigo, that is, fear of looking at or remembering the previous "bottom" I had hit while using and off my meds. As far as I was concerned, I did not have a mental illness. My girlfriend was afraid; our fights would lit-erally spill into the street and the police would frequently knock at my door. Ultimately, because of our fights and my continued drug use, she left me.

Years later, Mark shared a poem he had written about Dina, his girlfriend at the time.

> *A whirling ceiling fan and a dream catcher*
> *are all that is left of my life.*
>
> *I still feel you here.*
> *Your scent lingers on the clothes you never reclaimed.*
> *I smell them now and then:*
> *a hint of sweat mixed with lilac.*
> *Remember how you used to call my name*
> *(like you were afraid I was going to up and vanish one day)*
> *now, whenever you see me, you're just afraid.*
>
> *A whirling ceiling fan and a dream catcher*
> *are all that is left of my life.*
>
> *Winter's bite chills me to the bone*
> *the oven's heat is not enough to warm this place*
> *we once called home.*
> *Christmas is gone once again*
> *And my only resolution is erasing the sin of losing you.*

four

skyland encore

AFTER TWO MONTHS IN RESIDENCE at Skyland South, Mark was robust, clear eyed, and calm. Skyland South was a recently built section that housed clients in transition, looking toward independence. During our first visit, he showed us his tidy room and introduced us to his new friends. He did not bother to apologize for any of his earlier behavior, and we did not remind him of anything that had occurred. While I stood there watching Mark smile and make introductions, I realized I was livid. I experienced a wave of the same anger I had felt while cleaning up his last apartment mess. More than anything, I wanted him to apologize to me. I thought of all the furniture I had bought, all the money I had spent, and all the headaches I had nursed. But I said nothing. Instead, I tucked my anger away and acted the part of a caring mother. I was beginning to feel as if I had been doing the same thing over and over again expecting different results.

Pretense was not new to me. After our home invasion, after being raped, I had taught myself how to hide my feelings. I kept a ready smile and always looked for a room to slip into when my emotions threatened to get the best of me. In those days, I believed I knew how far to take any false story about my life. But one day, someone at the university asked me why I lived so far away from work. Without thinking, I replied, "I just love the country with all the cornfields. I love the geese flying overhead!" In that moment, I realized I was beginning to believe my own lie. We had been living within the Philadelphia city limits when our home was invaded. Afterward, we moved as far out of the city as possible.

After Mark became ill, I slipped back into the practiced mode of pretense, something I had done with acquaintances but never before with family. By pretending to accept Mark's topsy-turvy worldview even when he was on the edge of mania, I thought I could signal to him that my love and care had not changed. If Mark needed me to accept him as clairvoyant, I pretended I did. I even went so far as to pretend Mark was not suffering delusions when he said, "Can't you see that I know these things [about the world coming to an end] . . . and that I have been *chosen* by a higher power?"

"Of course, Mark. I understand," I replied. I hoped my simple acquiescence would calm him. Pretending to believe Mark's delusions was the only way I felt I could hold on to him and keep him from disappearing, alone, into his madness. Houston was the only one I ever let in on my little adjustments of the truth, and he never questioned my reasons.

Houston's conversations with Mark were seldom like mine. He always tried to maintain straightforward and honest dealings with his son. If Mark had told Houston about his so-called higher power, Houston would have said, "What in the world are you talking about, Mark?" Houston believed that with mental illness, make-believe could quickly become the real thing. He never entered into Mark's fantasies.

With our mentally ill son, we had no other choice except to respect each other in our individual strategies. I held on fiercely to the hope that somehow Mark would come back to us as the person we had always known.

Ten weeks into Mark's new sojourn at Skyland, Houston and I returned for another visit. Mark greeted us exuberantly, "Great to see you, Mom and Dad! Let me show you around," he said. This time, Mark seemed to understand his need for treatment. He explained his new medication regimen (something he had previously not been willing to share) and introduced us to the night nurse who dispensed medicine. He seemed genuinely pleased to see us, and, to my surprise and delight, he apologized for what he had put us through with the destroyed apartment.

"Hey, I'm really sorry about the mess I left behind. I had no idea it was so bad," he offered.

"Yeah, it was," I said, swallowing my impulse to elaborate. I did not want to create antagonism. As I think back now, I realize I probably should have taken that opportunity to voice my feelings of frustration and disgust. But time had passed, and I had regained my equilibrium. I was content that Mark was feeling good about himself. I could see a glimmer of his old self. Actually, I felt relief.

The next time I visited, I was no longer angry. Houston and I knew all of the residents by name, especially the ones who had become friendly with Mark. Mark seemed more centered than he had in many months, maybe even years. He talked and laughed easily. One young woman stood closer to him than to the others. I thought I saw them exchange glances, the kind of fleeting look that included no one else. She left the porch when we said our good-byes. As Houston and I drove away from Skyland, I turned to look back at Mark. We held eye contact as we waved. The young white woman I had noticed earlier came back onto the porch, nodded to Mark, and slipped her arm through his. "Houston, quick, take a look in your rearview mirror," I said, nudging him in the side. Silently, Houston and I watched the two of them.

new friends

MARK HAD BEEN LIVING IN Skyland South for five months. When I asked him if he had made any special friendships in his new home, he mentioned only one person: Michelle. In her generosity, Michelle had shared three or four pizza dinners with Mark when he was short on cash. He enjoyed talking with Michelle and described her as his new best friend. Remembering Skyland's strict policy forbidding residents to form couples, I impulsively said, "Is that a good idea, Mark? Spending time together alone? Don't forget the rules."

Mark was matter-of-fact in his response. "The other residents never invite us to eat with them. She's a really good person. Stop worrying, Mom."

During the next month, I kept up with Mark by telephone. He talked frequently about Michelle, often quoting advice she had given him, such as, "Mark, you have to let the past be the past. Aren't we here to start over?" Once in a while, Mark used similar phrases when talking with us.

Prior to her Skyland arrival, Michelle had been a successful computer software consultant with an Atlanta-based corporation. She owned a fully furnished two-bedroom condominium in the Buckhead area, on the outskirts of Atlanta. Her sister and mother had maintained the condo while she was being treated for bipolar disorder at Skyland Trail. Michelle's eventual plan was to move back to her condo once her rehabilitation was complete. Houston and I learned that Michelle's stay at Skyland would last only a bit longer. She was waiting for a group living arrangement as her next step toward resuming independence.

After hearing Michelle's plans for completing rehab, we secretly worried that Mark would insist on following her lead out of Skyland South. This would be premature since he had no apartment to return to and was moving at a different pace in his therapy. Almost immediately, we discovered that our concerns were real. Soon after Michelle moved into a group living arrangement, Mark began to talk incessantly about the freedom of communal living, hinting, of course, that it might be good for him, as well. Mark's therapist, aware of Mark and Michelle's intense relationship, decided Mark was ready to have a few more guarded freedoms. They gave him passes for off-campus meals and a later curfew. What a terrific preemptive move, we thought.

Mark and Michelle continued their relationship. They juggled Mark's passes for off-campus activities with evening dinners prepared by Michelle and her two housemates. Many of Mark and Michelle's so-called dates, however, were spent within the gardens of Skyland Trail since they each had limited budgets. During this time, Mark found a small job within the Skyland community as manager of a mobile coffee cart. The job paid a pittance, but he took pride in the money he earned selling cups of coffee. During his rounds, he also made more friends.

When Houston and I next visited Skyland, Mark took my hand and led me to the coffee-cart station, proud to show it off. I remember feeling sorry for my slow-moving son. Mark and Michelle talked constantly during this period. Mark told me that they even discussed whether Skyland would approve of their being therapeutic supports for each other, a buddy system that Skyland therapists had recommended for others. Michelle suggested, "You know my ups and downs, Mark. We spend so much time together. You know when I get depressed. You could be my early warning system, and I could be yours. Let's try it." So during the period of Michelle's group living arrangement and their frequent meetings, Mark and Michelle tried their new idea on their own.

After he had been living in the Skyland South facility for about seven months, Mark asked his dad, "What do you think about me living out on my own again in an apartment near Skyland with a group of guys, sorta like Michelle's arrangement? This time I wouldn't be alone."

When Mark asked, I felt the old, familiar churning in my stomach. Although I was proud of Mark's progress in treatment, his past episodes haunted me. I had not fully recovered from Mark's last psychotic break ten months earlier. I felt it was too soon for a move, but I said nothing. Houston asked me, "Why should we agree to this and put Mark in that situation again?" Houston told Mark how he felt, but despite Houston's stated objection to the move, Mark proceeded to make a formal request for communal living to his Skyland therapist. As it happened, Mark's bid for communal living coincided with Michelle's official and permanent release from Skyland Trail. She returned alone to her condo in Buckhead. Mark became her occasional visitor.

A few weeks later, in spite of our doubts, Houston and I traveled to Atlanta to discuss Mark's possible move into an off-campus, communal living arrangement. Sitting in a small, overly warm room, we tensely awaited the arrival of Mark's therapist. Once we were all assembled, Mark's counselor reminded us that Mark was not asking for permanent release. The Skyland administrators were inclined to allow him to move into a small group apartment. They would evaluate and supervise him regularly. Mark was pleased with the decision and hoped to make the transition toward total independence. He initiated discussion with us in an unusually calm and measured way. He had obviously given much thought to how he would present his plan to us. "Mom, Dad, I know the last time was really a bad scene. That won't happen again. I'm staying on my medication. Michelle and I have talked about helping each other live better. She's awesome. I know we are good together."

I was moved by the faith and confidence he seemed to have in Michelle. Mark was not quick to trust others. Houston and I knew that he needed our support in order to accept this new living arrangement. We felt we were witnessing a different son and agreed that Mark could move in with Pete, his friend at Skyland. In time, two other residents would join their communal living space. Mark agreed to remain in therapeutic day treatment and begin the process of looking for part-time employment. Vocational therapists at the treatment center would help Mark with this and would evaluate his progress. Mark consented to regular and unannounced supervision and agreed to submit regular reports on the status of his job hunting. Houston and I grew excited at the possibility of Mark's promotion to a semi-independent space, and we looked at available apartment units before leaving Atlanta. We felt confident that Mark would have the support he needed.

Within the week, as I was buying towels, dishes, and cleaning supplies for Mark's new place, a Skyland administrator called. He apprised us of a slight change in Mark's forthcoming living arrangements. Pete, Mark's friend, was not approved to move into communal living because he had some infractions on his chart, and therapists had been unable to locate another male client ready to live in a group situation. "But," they quickly offered, "Mark can move in alone until someone becomes eligible to join him."

Houston and I were unsettled by the news. Mark was unfazed. "I can move into the apartment alone, attend day treatment, find a job, and wait for Pete to join me," he said confidently. "I know I can do it, and I know Pete wants to do it. He thinks he'll be ready in a few months. I can do it, Mom and Dad. I know I can. Just give me a chance," Mark continued to plead.

Mark's quiet demeanor surprised us. We were even more startled when he suggested that the three of us discuss his bipolar disorder. "You need to know what is happening with me," he said. "And I guess I need to hear your side of things."

The next time Houston and I were in Atlanta, the three of us sat down together and began this conversation. Mark told us he understood the importance of taking his medication as prescribed and avoiding drugs and alcohol. He actually listened when I nervously told him, "Mark, money is running out, and we cannot take much more emotionally. We know you are ill, and it makes us profoundly sad. But you have to accept that you are ill. You must listen to your doctors, monitor yourself, and try to stay well. We are extremely tired, Mark. We can't do much more. We just can't keep going on the way we have been."

I expected anger, but Mark paused and said quietly, "But how will I know if I don't try again? Please, give me a chance. Michelle and I have talked about this, and she wants to help me. We can help each other."

Finally, Houston and I decided that if Mark's therapeutic team approved his living alone with increased supervision, we had no other objections. We agreed to provide another chance for Mark to live independently. He convinced us to try one more time.

Mark moved into his new apartment unit with some of the old furniture we had placed in storage. He needed a bed since Houston had discarded the mattress from Mark's last apartment. It had reeked of cigarette smoke, and Houston was certain Mark had used it as an ashtray. The two of them went in search of a new, but inexpensive, mattress and metal bed frame. When they returned, Houston sat with me on the outside stairway while Mark unpacked boxes inside.

It was still early in the day, but Houston was tired. He said, "That was one of the more bizarre shopping trips I've ever been on. Where we bought the mattress, the young black guy who waited on us was very nice. He asked Mark what kind of work he was in and where he was moving. Mark said openly, 'I have bipolar disorder, and I've been in rehab at Skyland Trail. I'm moving out on my own now. I need some things.' The salesman answered Mark with no hesitation, 'Man, that's so good. You're doin' the right thing. I congratulate you on that. I know some guys just can't make it.' " When Houston and Mark were leaving the store, Mark and the salesman shook hands as if they had known each other forever. The salesman gave Mark a hard pat on the back and said, "Stay strong."

The friendship between Mark and Michelle deepened, and they talked at least twice a day, always before bedtime. Michelle adored Mark's visits to her condo, and he arranged as many as he could. Mark told us that from time to time, Michelle reminded him to take his medication. "Never skip. I know you want to," she teased, "but don't skip!" She did not monitor his schedule, but she was adamant about Mark taking his prescribed medicine.

Mark's job hunt was challenging. He endured one retail interview after another. He tried a few jobs, but either the labor was too strenuous or the hours were too long. When he was not searching for work, Mark slept. The year progressed. Pete never arrived.

Our telephone conversations during Mark's semi-independence were uneventful, even pleasant. One night, Mark and I talked about the new movie *8 Mile*, starring the rapper Eminem. Mark asked, "Mom, did you see *8 Mile*? Wasn't it amazing?"

At first, I hesitated to answer. Houston and I had seen the movie, but my reaction had been negative. Carefully, I responded, "Yes, we did see *8 Mile*." Then the words just spilled out, "Mark! I don't know when I have seen anything so violent and unnecessary. How could you think I would like it? You know how I feel about rap. Just the hard bass beat of it disturbs me." Mark did not respond immediately. I thought to myself, Now what have I started?

He gave me time to take a breath, and then he calmly said, "Maybe, Mom, you went to the movie expecting to see only the violence. Maybe the soundtrack distracted you. I know there was misogyny, but did you get the real sense of the film, a saga about a poor white boy living in a trailer park—like living in the projects—looking for a way out? He was just as stuck as any black boy, and music gave him a road out. All that came through in the film. It's a film about class, Mom. You teach about class in your course, right? You were the one who told me to remember not all white people were well-off. As for the boy's rap, it was pretty good stuff." He smiled through the telephone.

Right there, mid-conversation, I realized that Mark and I were talking as we used to do before he became ill. During his teenage years, the two of us would playfully dissect and debate the merits of the latest Hollywood films. In this conversation, we were not in agreement, but by the end, I heard myself saying, "Well, maybe I will go back and see it again, Mark. Maybe I missed something." The following week, I saw the film again and realized that Mark had been astute in his assessment of the movie's realistic depiction of domestic violence and white poverty. I later used the film in my university teaching on gender, race, and violence.

home visit

FOR THANKSGIVING 2001, HOUSTON AND I invited Mark to North Carolina. He accepted with excitement. He immediately asked if he could bring Michelle. For an instant, I was surprised and then said eagerly, "Of course!" Later, I understood my hesitation; Mark had never asked to bring home anyone special for Thanksgiving or Christmas. I had never registered that fact until he asked.

Our Thanksgiving with Mark and Michelle was comfortable from the beginning. Michelle returned our sincere, "Welcome!" with a genuine smile and an extension of arms filled with packages wrapped for Christmas. Everything dripped with gold and silver ribbons. Her gifts included homemade cookies with names that made you want to open the tin and taste: hello dollies, cherry snowballs, chocolate chip shortbread cookie logs, and death by chocolate. I began sampling all of them. Houston and I invited Michelle and Mark into the living room and promised a later tour of the second floor. Mark had seen some of the earlier construction on the house, but this was his first visit to our newly completed home. I was so pleased that he was finally there.

Wanting to keep things simple before lunch, I had prepared a tray of crackers and cheese to nibble while we made conversation. I nervously asked the usual get-acquainted questions: "How was the drive? Was the traffic smooth? Would you like to settle down in your room? You must be hungry." As Michelle tried to answer all my questions in order, Mark went immediately to the kitchen to find drinks for everyone. I saw his smile as he passed by me. By the time he returned with glasses of iced tea, I had settled down a bit.

Houston and I thanked them for making the trip to North Carolina for the holiday. "While you are here," I said, "please make yourself at home." I meant it. For some reason, I instantly had good feelings about Michelle.

We moved into the dining room for a light lunch. This was the first time Mark had invited a female friend for an entire weekend, so I wanted to be particularly careful about what I said. I served up the various salads of shrimp, tuna, and chicken along with bread, cheese, fruit, and, of course, more iced tea. Michelle and Mark conversed easily, and Michelle filled us in on her plans for the Christmas holiday. Speaking of her niece and nephew in Atlanta, she said, "I think the children will spend part of the holiday time with their father, but I will still get a chance to make a Christmas celebration for them. I love doing that, and it helps my sister."

"Tell us more about the children," Houston responded. "Mark tells us that you are very close."

Michelle told us their ages and proudly proclaimed, "They are both great in school. Alan even made the honor roll this year."

"What about your niece?" I asked. "I bet you love having a little girl in your life."

"I do, and my sister lets me enjoy her whenever I want. Sometimes I feel like she's my own," Michelle smiled.

I enjoy watching guests at my table, even when I am often quiet myself. I was content with Mark and Michelle, feeling the relaxation unfold. They told us stories about the residents at Skyland Trail. Mark was still attending day sessions, and Michelle kept up with the happenings. Skyland residents were already preparing for their spring concert. Michelle spoke of one resident who "claims to play the trombone," but was not a certain pick for the concert. "He carries that horn around all the time, but do you think he can really play? His notes seem a little bit off to me," Michelle laughingly said. Then looking at us and elbowing Mark gently in the side, she said, "I've been trying to get Mark to read some of his poetry for the spring concert."

Mark smiled and simply said, "Not sure. Maybe."

After lunch, we took a brief walking tour of downtown Durham and the campus, stopping to look at our offices. I was proud to show off my large workspace with a window and air conditioner, things not always promised in a vintage academic building. We returned home in early evening and started cooking dinner. Mark and Michelle offered to help make the chili that would be our evening meal. Mark found the necessary utensils, and Michelle, without asking, picked up an apron and began organizing the chopping detail. They moved easily in the kitchen together. They talked and laughed as they worked, as if they were alone. Houston and I sat nearby in the television room, reading and relaxing to the soft hum from the kitchen. Michelle seemed to fit right in.

While we waited for the chili to simmer for dinner, everyone took a break. Mark and Michelle decided to take a walk around the neighborhood. Houston retreated to his e-mail, and I rested in a room near his study. I heard Mark and Michelle when they returned and proceeded to the den to stretch out on the rug. Their quiet brought such calm. I had not experienced this side of Mark in a very long time. The ring of the kitchen timer awakened me. After we shared chili and cornbread, we entertained ourselves with Trivial Pursuit, one of Mark and Michelle's house gifts. They must have practiced their game before arrival because they beat us royally.

The next afternoon at home, Michelle and I looked through family pictures, especially those of Mark growing up. She reminded me so much of myself when I first met Houston's parents, as she delightedly shouted, "Oh, look at this one. Isn't he so cute!"

Her exclamation brought Mark from the next room, with Houston trailing behind. They both began narratives to accompany the pictures in the album. Pointing to a snapshot of Houston trying to soothe two disgruntled six-year-olds, Mark chuckled, "Wasn't that the time Ricky and I argued about who got to the top of the museum steps first?" With Mark's nudge of memory, I recalled the day of our excursion to Philadelphia's Please Touch Museum and how excited Mark and his best buddy, Ricky, had been. In this moment of reminiscence, Michelle listened intently to details, watching Mark's every reaction. It was such a welcome change to feel so completely ordinary, sitting in our living room with our son and his girlfriend. Michelle brought a calm to our group.

Following this successful Thanksgiving visit, Michelle invited us to spend time with them in Atlanta in March. Houston and I were thrilled. We realized that this would be our first visit to Mark in Atlanta that was not necessitated by a crisis involving illness, jail, or rehab. We were actually invited to spend a relaxing weekend at Michelle's condo.

I worked hard to choose the right gift to take to Mark and Michelle. I finally settled on a colorful piece of pottery. When we arrived, it was clear that Michelle had prepared for our visit. The table was set for four, with fresh flowers. She gave us a tour of her well-appointed condo. We figured that Mark must have been spending most of his time there since Michelle had decorated her second bedroom in a Spider-Man theme for Jack. I could not help but compare her space to the apartment Mark had shared with Lisa and Jack only a few years prior. Lisa and Mark had lived in public housing. Jack and Lisa's daughter, Angela, had shared a sleeping space with them. Lisa and Mark's apartment had been clean, but their furniture had been covered with blankets and shawls to hide the shabbiness of the cushions. When I sat on their sofa, the coverlet had slipped off behind me, revealing a gaping hole. I remembered the look of embarrassment on Lisa's face.

Years later and a world apart, Houston and I stood in Michelle's beautiful living room admiring her African artifacts. Her couch was accented with silk brocade pillows. She blushed with pride when we complimented her taste.

further acquainted

ON THE FIRST DAY OF our visit, we spent hours relaxing with Michelle and Mark in the condo. Conversation was easy among the four of us. I was so pleased when Michelle began to tell us about the job she had held for five years with a well-respected computer firm. Before her illness struck, she had been a consultant and team captain for designing and updating software for companies and organizations in the United States and abroad. Travel had been an essential part of her job.

"The job seemed tailored for me," she said. "I didn't have to answer to anyone on the job site. I reported to my boss when I returned home to Atlanta. Plus, I only had to stay a few days in each place before I was off to the next. I could hide any feelings of depression, and my bouts of mania just helped me to look like a winner wherever I went." She added, "Of course, I didn't know then that I had a problem. I just loved the excitement of new challenges."

She then asked Houston and me about our university jobs. I was sure Mark had already told her more than she had wanted to know. I told her about one of my students who was writing for the *New York Times* and two others who had been writers for *Sex and the City*.

"I always love seeing their bylines or their names scroll across the television. I guess I was born to teach," I said. "I get excited each semester when I meet a new group. It's like having new recruits twice a year." As I talked, we all gravitated toward the kitchen. I asked Michelle about her possible return to the job she liked so much.

"My boss said he would hold the job for me," she said, "but I'm not sure I can handle the hours and the travel anymore. I think the long hours that I loved are not especially good for my condition. I always told myself that I would make vice president by the age of thirty. I had been promoted several times, and I was really on my way. Then bipolar knocked me down. I'm not sure what I'll do now. It all depends. I used to enjoy meeting all kinds of people. But now, since my break, I have a little problem with new people and crowds. They make me anxious, and I hate that."

For a moment she looked sad, but then gently changed the subject. She asked if we were hungry for lunch, and then said, "We can all make our own sandwiches right here."

Although Michelle and I were still getting to know each other, I felt a strong connection. I liked her casual manner and her honesty about her life, even the unpleasant parts of it. She told me that, in retrospect, she believed her job in the computer industry had suited her in many ways but had also contributed to her illness. "I didn't know then that I was suffering from bipolar disorder. I did my job well, and when I traveled, I enjoyed hanging out and drinking in the evenings with my coworkers. I could party late, work late, and still get up in the morning and hit the road. I didn't need much sleep. Once I got started, I just kept on going."

I asked her, "What happened once you really got sick?"

"After bipolar caught up with me, I couldn't hide anymore. It slowed me way down. I went into a deep depression, and I was hospitalized. I'd felt it coming on. I just didn't know what it was. Eventually, I ended up in Skyland Trail for about a year," she explained.

In spite of this, Michelle seemed centered and fundamentally OK with herself. I liked the fact that she could enjoy a good laugh.

She and Mark were setting out the ingredients for sandwiches when I heard her giggle. I turned to see them with their heads together. They had accidentally bought too little of the deli meat for lunch. Mark made a joke about who might want a lettuce and tomato sandwich, and we all agreed to help ourselves to "halfsie" sandwiches—half meat and half veggie. After we had spent a few hours together, I began to fathom the varying tones of Michelle's giggles, like one might learn the slight shift in a baby's cries. I was especially tuned into the sound of Michelle's contentment. I loved the way Mark touched her hair ever so gently when he was talking to her and thought no one was looking. They enjoyed the bliss of each other. The fact that they each had bipolar disorder did not reach into every aspect of their life. When they were together, the illness often seemed a world away.

In contrast, I worried about bipolar constantly. When Houston and I sat quietly, we worried about the possibility that both of them would get sick at the same time. What would we do? How could we help? When we returned to the hotel that night, we promised each other that in the presence of Mark and Michelle we would try not to dwell on the subject. I wanted to try to grab onto some of their hope and possibility. During this time, Mark wrote:

> *Even God smiles*
> *at knowing*
> *that no matter how dark the day*
> *through you*
> *the sun will find a way.*

Houston and I enjoyed our telephone exchanges with Mark; they were quiet yet informational. At one point, Mark told us that his favorite doctor, Dr. V., changed his medicine as soon as he discovered that Mark was not sleeping. The new medication worked well, and we appreciated Mark's willingness to communicate with us about this aspect of his life. It had not always been so. Mark was happy in his relationship with Michelle, and in turn, he seemed happier with us. He never ended a call without saying, "I love you." Mark was still attending Skyland treatment programs, and he continued to search for a job that would initially provide him with short workdays. Houston and I paid his rent and sent him money for living expenses.

Rest and minimal stress were important to Mark's well-being. I especially enjoyed listening to Houston's end of the conversation when he talked with Mark. Houston was so much more relaxed, and they seemed to be rediscovering the humor in their friendship. One night, I heard Houston laughing energetically on the telephone. I asked him what was so funny, and he sweetly waved me away, saying, "Nothing, really. Something Mark said reminded me of our old conversations when he was in college."

Mark and Houston shared one-phrase triggers to long-standing humor. In this instance, Houston had simply asked Mark, "How's your day?"

Mark had quickly responded, "Just waitin' for the zombies to hit the window and the dead crow to drop." The exchange had sent Houston into peals of laughter, remembering their mutual love of zombie horror movies. I recalled earlier days when Houston and Mark had howled with laughter at some story one of them had recounted. Houston's stories were always detailed, with twists and turns, building to the punchline, while Mark's were usually cryptic with dialogue and appropriate inflections. Sitting with the two of them had been great fun, but I also remembered that their delight in each other was as passionate as their anger could sometimes be.

We visited Atlanta three months later as the summer heat descended. We were delighted this time that Jack could spend more days with us at Michelle's condo. He loved his Spider-Man room, and his affection for Michelle had only deepened. He sometimes forgot and called her "Mommy." I saw him rush over to the two of them and say, "Let's do something fun," as he grabbed hold of them, each by one leg. Since the weather was warm, we spent hours splashing our feet in the pool of the condominium complex. Jack was quite a good swimmer and enjoyed our praise as he attempted to dive off the side. We thought his splashing superb. Houston and I loved the attention of a grandson.

During our visit, Michelle, Mark, and Jack treated us to a day at Stone Mountain State Park, a huge Atlanta tourist attraction in the greener outskirts of the city. There were miles of walking paths, carnival rides, cotton candy, ice cream cones, popcorn, and clowns. At carefree times like these, you persuade yourself that surely your friend back home will enjoy a daily journal with I LOVE GEORGIA on the cover. I also discovered I was not the only one with a fondness for hot dogs. Jack's eyes lit up when I suggested we stop for one. I could not remember the last time I had been so relaxed, as we watched jugglers and ate our snacks. Mark suggested to Jack that they find an area to pitch softballs with his new catcher's mitt. Jack let out a shout of agreement, and the three guys took off in search of an open space.

Mark and Michelle had visited the park previously and described the fireworks we would get to see later in the day. We had some time before the display would begin, so Michelle and I found a good viewing spot to set down our picnic blanket. As I helped Michelle empty the shopping bags filled with dinner, I realized what a lavish meal she had prepared for the five of us, enough to feed us for days: broiled crispy chicken, deviled eggs, potato salad (just they way I like it with loads of mayonnaise), lettuce and tomato, fruit salad, homemade cookies, and lemonade. Everything was neatly encased in its own plastic container for the return trip home. We had a tablecloth, napkins, plates, cups, forks, and knives. Michelle had forgotten nothing. I was impressed. We talked as we worked. As I watched Michelle, I thought of my mother and smiled. My mother would serve a similar picnic meal, and she, too, would have used perfectly sized plastic containers. Michelle appeared as self-assured as my mother always was. Perhaps Mark sensed the likeness, too.

"I want you to meet my mother one day. I think you'd like each other," I said. "She and Mark were so close as he was growing up. He turned to her with all his secrets, and whenever he got peeved with me, he ran to her," I said with delight. "She was always available for him. You are special to Mark as well, so I think the two of you should meet."

Michelle answered me with a hug. "My sister and I were close like that," she said.

As Michelle and I relaxed, I suddenly realized the light was fading. "We need to call the guys back in. We need to eat before we can't see," I said waving to them. I could see Mark, Houston, and Jack in the distance still throwing the ball. More and more people streamed into our area for the fireworks until we were sitting shoulder to shoulder with adults and children. Toddlers were running and leaping over dinner plates. When I looked back, the entire hillside was packed with people who had gradually filled in the spots left by earlier picnickers. With the return of Mark, Houston, and Jack, we settled down and consumed a splendid meal. Jack loved the fireworks, and we all nibbled homemade cookies in the dark.

Once the fireworks finished, we joined the crowds streaming back to the parking lot. Slowly we walked, heavy from a day in the sun. Jack was half asleep on Mark's shoulder. We dropped Mark, Michelle, and Jack at the condo, and Houston and I returned to our hotel. We promised to visit the following afternoon, bringing lunch with us.

Our next day together in Atlanta was even more relaxing than the first. We were primed for a good time. The only one missing was Jack; he went home to be with his mother. Once we had all settled in the living room, Mark and Michelle began to reminisce about their short romance. "Do you remember when I first noticed you, Mark?" Michelle teased.

"Of course I remember. It's when I first noticed you!" Mark answered.

"No, you are all wrong," she shot back. "Because I smiled at you more than once, and you paid me no attention. One time you just went on talking to someone else like you didn't even know who I was. I had been checking you out for a long time," she said confidently.

"Really? You mean before we actually talked, you had been lookin' at me?" Mark asked, grinning widely. "You should have let me know," he said.

Michelle just laughed, "That's OK, hon. I thought it was cute. You didn't have a clue."

Reflecting on their relationship, Michelle said thoughtfully, "Mark, it's so good we didn't meet earlier. You know, we probably would not have been ready to meet. In fact, I know I wouldn't have been ready to meet anyone. I was in really bad shape."

Mark countered, "Me too. I couldn't even keep a plant alive!"

They talked softly but not secretively. "I get goose bumps," Michelle said, "when I think we might have missed each other." Then, with only a brief pause, she turned to Houston and me and said, "I guess we have something to tell y'all." Houston and I perked up.

"Mark and I have decided to get married," she calmly announced as they exchanged glances.

"Wow! That's terrific!" I said.

Immediately, Houston chimed in, "When is the big day?"

Michelle responded right away, "Not for a year. We have lots to do. We want a big wedding, and we have to save money. By the end of the year, Mark will have a job, and he will be done with Skyland."

Houston and I got to our feet and gave them congratulatory hugs. "Sounds really good," Houston said, nodding.

Picking my words carefully, I said, "Tell us more." In my mind's eye, I saw Mark still in Skyland Trail without a job. It was difficult for me to process a marriage and new beginning when he had not yet finished fulfilling the therapeutic protocols to get well, stay sober, and find employment. Mark smiled quietly, obviously pleased that Michelle was so happy. I let my worry reside elsewhere. Houston and I remained focused on the good news.

"What type of wedding are you planning? And where will you live?" we asked, in turn.

Michelle filled in the details. "We would only live in Atlanta or nearby because Jack lives here with his mom, and we need to be near Jack. He's kinda like my kid already," she smiled.

Mark agreed and added, "The condo is big enough for the three of us. If we need help with our bipolar disorder, our doctors are here, and so is Skyland Trail."

Michelle told us that they would probably look to buy a home in another year. We just stood in the middle of Michelle's living room, smiling. We had never experienced this before. When Mark and Lisa married, they had eloped. They had barely made plans for the following week. Mark and Michelle stood close together with fingers interlocked. Clearing his throat, Mark said, "We want you to know that you are very important to us. We want you and Beth [Michelle's mom] to stay close to us and remain part of our life. Even though we have doctors, we want you to tell us if you think things are not right with us. We will do everything to keep each other well, but we still really need you."

Michelle nodded in agreement. Houston and I were moved by this unanticipated moment. We agreed to help them succeed in their life together. It was like taking a vow.

Back at the hotel, Houston and I were contemplative and quiet. "I'm worried. Mark doesn't even have a job," Houston stated.

"But did you see their faces?" I asked. "They were so happy with each other!" In spite of my very real happiness for them, I could not help remembering Mark's last psychotic episode. Houston reached out for my hand. How would they be able to sustain a life together with little money and the seemingly insurmountable health challenges they faced?

a wedding

WE RETURNED TO NORTH CAROLINA and slowly began to tell our friends about Mark's upcoming wedding. Doing so helped us absorb the news ourselves. We believed that Mark and Michelle had been wise to choose each other, and we were delighted our family would soon include an amazing daughter. Mark kept us abreast of his continuous job interviews. After the disappointment of one particular rejection, he talked to us about the possibility of going back to finish his doctoral studies. I tried to convince him that he did not need the stress of taking classes and exams. "Don't give up trying to find a profession, Mark. Eventually, you'll find a space where you feel comfortable," I insisted. He accepted my comfort for the moment, but every so often he returned to the idea of graduate school.

The rejections he received while job searching continued to upset him. One day, Mark called, and I could hear the despair in his voice. He started in on a story with no preface, "When I got there, there were all these guys lined up, and we were looking at each other kinda like, 'So, what are *you* here for?' Some of them didn't want to engage, but I thought that was a good sign for me since I never have a problem engaging, and I thought maybe the manager would see the difference in us, you know? And I was lookin' good, Mom. I wore that new shirt you sent me. I know I was more on the ball than most of those other guys 'cause they didn't go right up to the manager with outstretched hand like I did, know what I mean?" He chuckled. "You know, the way Granddad Houston used to say in his serious voice, 'Look 'em in the eye, Mark, and get your hand out there for a shake. If they're short, get down on their level. But look 'em in the eye.'" Mark laughed again. "I've been thinking of Granddad a lot these days," he said and then trailed off.

By the end of his story, Mark told us the manager had liked his interview and asked him to return for another chat. During the second session, however, the manager told him, "Your resume looks terrific. But your background with the jail time and the mental illness, well, that doesn't look so hot. Can't do it." I realized I had been holding my breath while I listened to Mark's story. He was incredibly disappointed. Years later, he told me how depressed he had gotten after each dismissal.

A few months later, Mark triumphed. He called to tell us he had gotten a job as a salesman with a vitamin and supplement store in Atlanta. Mark had known the good news for about two weeks but said he "wanted it to be a done deal before I called you."

"Can you believe it? I got a job! A job!" he shouted into the telephone. I could picture him slamming high fives into the air and smiling ear to ear. Mark, Houston, and I were so excited that we began to talk over one another. Mark would start work in one week, and he would receive benefits after a probationary period of four months. The store where he would work was located near his Skyland Trail apartment. It seemed almost perfect. But when Mark called at the end of his first week, the sound of exhaustion had replaced his excitement.

"I'm not sure if I can do this, Mom," he sighed.

"Yes, you can," Houston and I said, almost simultaneously. "Just remember to get plenty of rest and take your medicine."

Working six-hour days, week after week, with only one day off in seven was more than a challenge for Mark. We prayed a lot during those early weeks. Mark eventually settled into the job, but he continued to fight fatigue and depression. His therapist coached him through the first few months. With the shadow of jail and probation still haunting him, Mark knew he had to persevere.

After he had worked four months, Mark's job as retail sales-man became permanent. He was overjoyed when his health ben-efits kicked in. The benefits covered Jack, and, after marriage, they would cover Michelle. He felt immense relief. Mark's next concern was getting officially released from Skyland Trail. He consulted with his criminal attorney about his court-imposed probation. He learned that if he had proof of permanent residence, a bona fide job, successful completion of rehab at Skyland Trail, and someone to act as his guardian for the three remaining years of his proba-tion, the law would allow him to complete the probation period while living alone, with no further hospitalization. For the next three years, he would have to make regular monthly visits to city hall to confirm his place of residence and place of employment. Further, he would have to submit to random drug tests and prove that he was seeing a psychiatrist on a regular basis.

Houston and I agreed to be guardians for Mark until his mar-riage to Michelle. Their condo would become his permanent address. Mark now had a full-time job. His therapists at Skyland Trail documented the length of his inpatient residence and semi-independent living. They verified that Mark had fulfilled the requi-site number of months in therapy and that he was drug-free. With a stroke of the pen, Mark's therapist released him back into our world. I still worried that all the moments of success might simply unravel.

Michelle and Mark turned to their wedding plans. They had been trying to find a place for the ceremony and the celebration afterward. Finally, in Roswell, Georgia, a suburb of Atlanta, they found what they thought was perfect: Primrose Cottage, a charm-ing vintage home that specialized in weddings and receptions. Michelle designed lavender and white invitations and later selected lilies and baby orchids as flower arrangements for the table decora-tions. The cottage itself had large rooms and sumptuous couches, providing ample space for their fifty invited guests to move comfortably throughout the rooms for food and conversation. There was a small, glassed-in area set aside for dining and dancing.

In March 2004, Mark and Michelle exchanged marriage vows on a dais bedecked with flowers. It was Michelle's idea to have a garden wedding. Michelle wore a floor-length gown with layers of white tulle, and Mark wore a black tuxedo with a grey striped vest. Houston, his best man, wore the same tuxedo, and Michelle's sister, her matron of honor, wore a lavender gown that touched the grass. Jack was a ring bearer. He and his cousin, Alan, carried two rings to the dais on tiny pillows. Jack loved being dressed in a tuxedo like his dad. Michelle's six-year-old niece, dressed in volumes of white, tossed flowers along the grass. Houston and I walked together, followed by Michelle's mother and stepfather. Michelle and her dad completed the procession.

As Mark and Michelle recited their vows, Michelle's sister set free hundreds of butterflies. A surprised gasp rose from nearby guests as a wave of color fluttered into the air. The unexpected beauty of the moment made me search for tissues. For once in a very long time, I was not weeping because of illness. Not long after his wedding, Mark wrote the following poem:

> *Second chances*
> *to grab hold again,*
> *rare as kept secrets,*
> *give hope like rebirth*
> *and aromatic life*
> *fill air fresh with memory*
> *of the trauma of ice,*
> *frigid winds and naked branches.*
>
> *Laughs return to me*
> *like geese taking eager*

flight home
after southern vacations,
squirrels' hectic dances
around trees
are the only hint of mania left,
and I am free
from the wanton grip
of the illusions spun
within the slums
of my soul
and the mind's darkest
corridor's sadistic tricks
like delusions of warm snow
or a cold sun –
    Second chances
make me certain now
forever's just begun.

jobs, career, and family

MARK WENT BACK TO HIS job at the vitamin and supplement store once he and Michelle returned from their honeymoon in Hawaii. When I called Mark one evening, I heard Michelle giggling in the background. I quickly apologized for interrupting and said, "I can call back later if you want."

Mark laughed, saying, "It's OK, Mom. We were playing a board game, and Michelle just beat me, that's all."

"Hi, Mom!" I heard Michelle yell. I asked Mark how things were going at his job.

"Great. I have so much more energy after relaxing on the beach for a week," he replied. "The extra rest was good for me. Yesterday at work, I sold fifty-five dollars' worth of rewards cards, the most of any sales associate in the store!" he told me proudly. Mark delighted in the once-a-month promotional day. He regularly outsold other employees. His customers earned points, and he got bonuses. I remembered a similar members' day sale at Encore Books in Philadelphia from the days when Mark lived with us in the summer of 1997. He outsold the other employees then, too. Mark still loves the art of the sale. It gives him an adrenaline rush.

When he first began working as a sales clerk, his job provided him with two paychecks a month and a way to support his family. He did not consider it a career path and was still searching for alternatives, especially academic ones. The longer Mark stayed in the retail job, however, the more he grew to appreciate it. He looked for ways to make his work life more satisfying. He made an effort to become familiar with the likes and dislikes of his customers. He told me about one client, for example, who disliked vitamins with a strong smell. After Mark found him a more appealing product, the man became a regular customer.

When I visited Mark at work ("his store" as he began to refer to it), I met Don, a young employee who Mark had trained. Mark called him a coworker he could trust. He even told Don about his bipolar disorder. When Don talked to me that day, he only had words of admiration and praise for Mark: "He really knows this store. He's taught me so much."

That same day, I heard Mark explaining to a customer the possible side effects of a strength-enhancing supplement, and I was taken aback by his knowledge. At one point, I heard him say to the customer, "I'm not quite sure of that, but I can find out for you." Mark came back with a massive product catalogue and flipped with familiarity through hundreds of pages as he continued to consult with the customer. I had no idea Mark knew as much as he did about the general stock in the store. I was impressed.

At home, their wedding joy lingered on. Mark and Michelle had fun calling each other "Mr. and Mrs. Baker" and even referring to Jack as "our son" when they were in the grocery store and other shoppers could hear them. Jack thought that being a family was marvelous; eventually he began calling Michelle "Mommy Michelle." Jack was living with Mark and Michelle full-time now and visiting with his mother on some weekends and holidays. Mark and Michelle had hinted on several occasions that they were considering the idea of having children together. Months before the wedding, I had overheard Michelle say to Mark, "I've always wanted to have children of my own, and there is so much good in us, Mark."

Now, in the contentment of their marriage, they had begun to think about moving from Michelle's condo into a larger space in a child-friendly neighborhood. Michelle sought our advice about selling her condo, and Mark asked if I thought a new neighborhood should have a communal swimming pool. "Jack loves to swim," he reminded me. I got caught up in their excitement and found myself looking on the Internet for Atlanta real estate with pools and play equipment. I loved hearing about their dreams for the future.

Early one evening, Mark called with a sparkle in his voice. "Hi, Mom," he said. "We have some news for you. Put Dad on the line." I envisioned Michelle already leaning into the phone. I could hear her soft laughter. Houston had barely said hello when Mark announced, "Michelle's pregnant! We're going to have a baby."

I think our startle responses kicked in. Houston and I were quiet. Mark asked, "Are you still there? Isn't this great?" Houston and I looked at each other with raised eyebrows.

"Wow! Congratulations! You caught us off guard," I answered. "I guess we were not expecting things to move so fast. When's the baby due?" I smiled into the phone. At that moment, I realized I had been secretly hoping that Mark and Michelle would wait a few more years before starting a family.

When Houston and I hung up, I said to him, "This news calls for a glass of wine. Let's talk." Houston was just as unsettled as I was about the news of a baby.

"I don't see how they can have a child without planning ahead financially, do you?" he asked.

I agreed but told him, "Their financial instability is not my worst fear. Given Mark's and Michelle's challenges with bipolar disorder, I'm scared that some form of the disorder will show up later in the children. I read that there's a one in ten chance of bipolar disorder manifesting in the children of parents with the disorder. A few months ago, I sent Mark a copy of the Mondimore book *Bipolar Disorder: A Guide for Patients and Families*. Do you think they read it?"

Houston shook his head, saying, "I really don't know what to say, Charlotte. I thought we would have a few more years before we had to think about these issues."

Sadness reverberated in Houston's words. We were both concerned about Mark's and Michelle's long-term health challenges and the ways in which they might impact their responsibilities as parents. We worried about the well-being of our unborn grandchild and, at the same time, felt guilty discussing their intimate life as a couple. We acknowledged our feelings of helplessness to each other.

Michelle saw her physician right away and gradually weaned herself off lithium and Depakote. We learned that those drugs were potentially toxic for a developing fetus. Her doctor prescribed a different treatment for anxiety and depression and monitored her throughout her pregnancy. I worried that Michelle's body would react negatively to the absence of lithium, an essential medication for managing bipolar disorder. Her doctor explained that the dramatic shift in hormones during pregnancy helps to stabilize mood swings in some women. This information soothed my worries.

Michelle arranged for her obstetrician, her psychiatrist, and her therapist to work with her in tandem. Mark made sure that Michelle ate balanced meals regularly, and he encouraged her to exercise. At her obstetrician's suggestion, Michelle went to bed early. Jack was Michelle's constant companion, as soon as he got in from school. "Want a peanut butter sandwich?" he would ask, and Michelle dutifully obliged. Houston and I were very pleased that Michelle managed to remain healthy during the nine months of her pregnancy.

Michelle was four and a half months pregnant when Mark telephoned to say that they had found a single-family home in a community about forty minutes from downtown Atlanta. The house was partially built, so they would be able to choose their hardwood flooring and kitchen cabinets. They were ecstatic. "We've seen about thirty houses, and this one is the best, hands down," Mark told me excitedly. The house had three bedrooms and an ample backyard. The community had couples with young families. They immediately put Michelle's condo up for sale.

The same week, Mark told us that he had decided to apply for the newly posted job of assistant manager at the vitamin and supplement store where he was working. Houston and I inhaled deeply.

"Whoa," I said to Houston that evening. "This all seems a bit manic to me. Aren't they moving too fast?" Houston agreed with my concern.

I asked Mark why he was looking to shift jobs at this particular moment. "I'm feeling healthy, and Michelle seems happy," he said. He mentioned that Dexter, his manager, had been asking him for weeks to open the store in the morning and close it in the evening, a cherished task among employees because it signaled trust and loyalty. Mark thought this was a good moment to apply for the position since the notice of its vacancy had just appeared. As Mark spoke, I began to relax. He did not sound manic at all. I knew Mark liked his job, and Dexter appreciated him as an employee. If he gained the job as assistant manager, he would have even more accountability. He would deposit the day's accumulated cash at the local bank's night teller and hire new personnel. His working hours and pay would increase. Mark assured us that he had talked with his therapist about his possible job change. When he told us a few weeks later that he had earned the promotion to assistant manager of the store, I was not at all surprised.

Three months later, I realized I had relaxed too soon.

The telephone rang one evening at midnight. I answered and heard Michelle whisper nervously, "Mom, Mark is acting strange." Michelle told me that she had gotten a call the day before from

Mark's manager, who was extremely upset and had abruptly asked to speak with Mark. When Mark closed the store the night before, he had failed to lock the outside door to the store in the mall. Dexter was furious. Mark admitted to forgetting and apologized profusely. He told his manager that he had successfully deposited the entire profits of the day in the nighttime bank drop.

"I did that right," he told Dexter.

"We will have to see about this," Dexter answered. "These are grounds for letting you go, you know. This is a business."

Michelle was inconsolable. "What will we do, Mom, if Mark loses his job? He's edgy, and he won't sit still. He can't go to work like that."

Mark was also acting peculiarly at home. Michelle told me, "Two days ago, he accused me of talking secretly to the repairman who was fixing the leaks under the sink. The man was only here a few minutes, and Mark said I was flirting with him! Can you imagine? Mark's becoming increasingly suspicious of me for no reason. I've been trying to get him to go to the doctor, but he won't do it. We've been trying to tell each other when the other slips out of a routine. I've told Mark that he's imagining things, but I don't think he can hear me."

Half asleep, I answered, "You've got to persuade Mark to see the doctor, Michelle, and you should probably go with him." I quietly listened as she described Mark's strange tirade about the city of Atlanta not giving them money to replace the floor in the kitchen of Michelle's condo.

"I've tried to tell him that it's not the city's fault that the pipe under the kitchen sink burst. I have to pay for it. It's my property. I've told him that over and over," she sighed. Just my listening seemed to calm her. I sympathized with her so much.

"Get some sleep, Michelle. We'll talk later in the day," I said.

When Michelle called again, I could hear Mark in the background. It sounded like he was haranguing her, but his words were not intelligible. I was not sure he had slept at all, and I understood why Michelle was unnerved. Michelle kept urging him to see his psychiatrist, and Mark finally agreed. They went together to the appointment. The doctor increased Mark's dosage of Depakote, tweaked his other medication, and reminded him that he needed to get proper rest, at least eight to ten hours each night. Over the next two weeks, Mark responded well to the increase in his medicine, and his anxious behavior subsided. As he settled down, they both became more aware of each other's need for regular rest. Mark joined a new gym and tried to exercise twice a week until his hours increased at the store. Then he had no free time. Michelle's pregnancy continued uneventfully.

With the help of Michelle's sister and a few friends, Mark and Michelle (in her sixth month of pregnancy) moved into their new home in the community of Powder Springs, on the outskirts of Atlanta. The furniture from Michelle's condo fit perfectly into their new home. Michelle's mother made curtains for most of the windows in the house, and Houston and I helped them buy a crib and rocker for the nursery. Mark and Michelle bought clothes for the new baby and started picking out colors to paint the nursery.

I was completely surprised one afternoon when Michelle called out of the blue to invite me to witness the birth of their baby. "You didn't have that chance with your first grandchild," she explained. "I want you to be there for this one." I was incredibly touched by Michelle's generosity. I had never thought of witnessing my grandchild's birth. I had envisioned myself huddled next to a telephone, waiting for the news.

"Wow! Thank you, Michelle. How can I thank you enough? You sure know how to make a grandmom happy. I'll be there!" In that instant, I felt I had been given a daughter.

Before sleep that night, I said to Houston in the dark, "You know, I think Mark and Michelle will make fine parents. When children have problems later on in life, you just deal with it."

I caught myself smiling when I thought of seeing my grand-child enter the world. With my own words, I patted myself calm and decided to take a deep breath and let the future unfold. Houston and I decided to work on being good grandparents. The very next week, I began shopping like there was no tomorrow. I appeared so often in the Macy's infant department that I became friends with the salesperson. One afternoon, she looked at me and said, "Back so soon?" We both laughed. Browsing the aisles of baby clothing brightened my mood considerably. I began to mark days off the calendar leading up to Michelle's due date, and I loved saying that I was shopping for my daughter. Even the shadow of a stroller in the mall now turned my head.

The day before Michelle's doctors induced labor, Houston and I traveled to Atlanta. Michelle had invited Houston to be present for the birth, as well. When we arrived at the hospital the next day, I took a short tour. The soft green and blue walls created a relaxing space in which to wait. The nurses wore colorful smocks printed with flowers or cartoon characters. The doctor predicted that the birth would occur around 3:00 AM, and it was only 7:00 PM. Houston and I decided to leave and find a place nearby to eat dinner. We planned to return about ten o'clock to sit with Mark and Michelle, watch game shows on TV, and distract Michelle from her labor pains.

As we returned from dinner, searching leisurely for a parking space in the crowded hospital garage, Houston's cell phone rang. It was about 9:30 PM. Houston answered, and Mark asked, "Dad, where are you and Mom right now?"

When Houston told him, Mark shouted, "Dad, run! Run as fast you can! The baby's coming—right now!!"

We parked in some slanted fashion, creating a new, probably illegal, parking space, and took off on foot. We ran like two teenagers, brushing past people in the hospital corridors, stopping only to ask for directions to the birthing unit. Out of breath, we burst through the door to Michelle's room and found everyone in whisper mode. The nursing team broke into laughter when they saw the wide-eyed grandparents erupting onto the scene. We calmed each other and shed our coats. Michelle was in the stirrups, waiting for her command to "Push!" We murmured encouragement and blew her kisses. We gave Mark a thumbs-up. Houston grabbed the camera, having been given the task by Michelle to take pictures. "Only appropriate ones, Dad," she smilingly told him.

At 10:05 PM on January 18, 2005, Eric was born with eyes wide open. Michelle had wanted a daughter, but once she saw Eric, it no longer mattered. At the exact moment of his birth, my gaze was fastened onto the hands of the doctor as she readied for the catch. I was not sure what to expect, but I knew something phenomenal was about to happen. When I saw the top of his head, the crowning, I was transported. All sound ceased. The room had no one in it but me. Eric's final, gentle turn seemed like the most exquisite pirouette I had ever seen. I began to clap. I wanted to shout, "Do it again!"

Just after the birth, Jack arrived with Michelle's mother in time to see his new brother being swaddled against the chill of the room. Jack bounced excitedly on his toes and stared in disbelief at his new little brother. "Can I touch him?" Jack chirped. Once Eric was clean and had been properly examined and tested, the nurses allowed Jack to stroke his new brother and hold his fingers. Houston snapped pictures of their first meeting. The nurses beamed their congratulations. Minutes later, I breathed in the smell of my new grandson as I held him for the first time.

Houston and I helped Mark bring Michelle and Eric back home. Eric's nursery was piled high with plush animals, wrapped gifts, and mounds of diapers. The nursery welcomed him into a fairyland of animals that Michelle had drawn or delicately pasted around the walls. Her mother planned to stay a few days longer. We returned to Durham. Houston and I had baby announcements of our own to address and mail.

Eric was a good baby. He slept often and cried only when he was hungry. Michelle enjoyed nursing and holding him. She slept when he slept. He seldom left her arms. Mark got up each morning with Jack, prepared his breakfast, and took him to the school bus. Then Mark's workday began with his job at the vitamin and supplement store. Three months quietly passed.

april madness

APRIL ARRIVED WITH A VENGEANCE.

Michelle's telephone voice was calm, as usual, "Mom, please, I want you to do nothing. I can handle this." I held my breath as she continued to speak. "I just wanted you and Dad to know in case I need you later. Remember, we promised we would tell you if anything went wrong?"

Trying to remain composed, I asked, "What happened, Michelle?" I beckoned to Houston to come sit near me.

"Mark is missing. I haven't spoken to him all day," she said. "He left for work around noon, but he didn't answer the store phone when I called. He's not answering his cell phone either. And there's more. He hasn't slept in days and has been pacing around the house. He's been mumbling to himself and making faces!"

"Michelle, why didn't you call us?" I blurted.

"I thought he'd snap out of it," she answered. "But he's getting worse. Last night he thought he saw ghosts, and he started taking pictures of them to show us. It scared Jack. Jack keeps staring at his dad and clinging to me." She began to cry, "I'm so tired. I've had to stay awake to watch him."

"Don't you think you should call his doctor?" I asked.

After a rather long pause, Michelle said, "I've been trying to tell Mark what's happening to him and to us. I keep saying, 'You have to call your doctor,' but he won't do it. He keeps telling me that I'm the one who's crazy. He thinks I'm trying to hurt him. But, Mom, you know I would never hurt Mark." At that moment, what I really wanted to do was hold Michelle in my arms and make everything better for her.

Houston and I called Michelle back that night and offered a solution. We were concerned for her safety and that of our grandchildren. We said, "If you don't feel safe in the house with Mark, we want you to take Jack and the baby and go to a motel. You can call us when you get there, and we will cover your stay with our credit card. Please take some time to think about this and call us back." We waited, and within the hour, Michelle called.

"Are things better?" we asked.

"I've been agreeing with everything he says," Michelle told us. "I don't know what else to do. He gets upset if I cross him. Your idea is the right thing. I think I should take the kids and leave for the night." I heard fear in her voice. Michelle called when she and the children were in place at a nearby motel. Houston and I went to bed but did not sleep.

The next day, I called Mark at work. When he answered the store phone, his voice was calm and professional: "Good afternoon. Georgia First Mall. Mark speaking."

"It's Mom," I said, and immediately I heard his slight intake of breath. "How're things going with you?" I asked.

He was careful, but not overly so. He began a litany: "Michelle's got real problems. She's nursing and doesn't want to wean the baby. It's been three months already, and she won't wean the baby. Everything's about the baby! She won't listen to me. She never puts the baby down, and as long as she's nursing, she doesn't take her lithium. Now that's a problem!"

He stopped abruptly. I was rattled by all the new information, as well as Mark's displeasure with Michelle. I suggested that Michelle's doctor should be able to help them. In response, Mark repeated his exact story. Finally without resolution, I said a quick good-bye. My heart was pounding. I knew things were not right. I had no idea about Michelle's medication schedule or her nursing demands. Mark's demeanor on the phone disturbed me.

When Houston came home, I gave him a detailed account of my conversation and reminded him that neither of us had ever witnessed the symptoms of Michelle's illness. "Did you know she was still not taking her lithium?" When he shook his head no, I said, "Suppose she's having a meltdown. We would never know." A feeling of uselessness overtook me. "I don't know what else to do! There're just too many people to keep track of. I can't do this anymore!"

Houston reached over and rubbed my back, and for several minutes, I let him. For the first time, I felt caught in the dilemma we had feared: Mark and Michelle possibly exhibiting symptoms of bipolar disorder at the same time. Houston said quietly, "I got this one. Don't worry."

Houston called our therapist and asked her to squeeze us into her schedule the next day. Michelle continued to call Mark throughout the night on his cell, with no response. The following morning, she left the motel and took Jack to school, trying to keep his routine unchanged. She returned home only to discover all the window blinds fully open and all the lights turned on throughout the house. Mark was nowhere in sight.

"I know he's manic and in trouble," Michelle said. "I know it," she repeated. Mark had strewn the children's toys around the yard. He had disassembled some of them. "He's delusional. He probably took them apart because he thought they were a threat to him. I've seen that behavior before," she said. "He's scared, Mom. I'm going out to look for him." Michelle put the baby in the car and drove through areas she thought Mark might go. She drove for about an hour and continuously tried to reach him by telephone. Still, he did not pick up.

When Michelle returned home again to feed the cat, she was surprised to bump into Mark rummaging through closets in the house. His eyes were glazed over, and he seemed disoriented. He had removed their family pictures from the wall in the hallway, and he had put boxes of photos out by the curb for trash pickup. He continued to throw out their belongings as he went through the closets. Michelle saw a video camera and an old pink cell phone of hers among the personal belongings that Mark had flung in the trash.

When she spoke to Mark and he literally grunted back at her, she got in the car, locked the doors, and settled the baby in his carrier. She decided to leave and return home later. However, when Mark saw Michelle pulling out of the driveway, he jumped into his car and swerved out of the driveway just behind her. In a few blocks, Michelle realized that Mark was following her. Every turn she made, he made. When she sped up, he did also. After a few miles, Michelle decided to go back home. She pulled into their driveway and called 911. She asked for the emergency medical service to come and take Mark to the nearest hospital. "I knew Mark would never hurt us," she said, "but I thought we should be in a safe space just in case he didn't know who we were."

Michelle called me from the car and told me what was happening. "Mark's completely gone," she said. I waited with Michelle on the telephone until the EMS arrived. I could hear her telling them that she was fine but that Mark was mentally ill and needed help. "Please don't hurt him. He doesn't like being touched," she said. I heard the officer ask Mark if he would voluntarily get into the emergency medical van. He complied.

Michelle hurriedly spoke into the phone: "I have to go, Mom. I'm following them to the hospital. Mark thinks I'm out to get him. Somewhere in there, I hope he knows I love him."

Mark remembered the incident and much later wrote the poem "Abandonment":

Top lock's foreign.
And there's a bomb in the driveway!
(really just a suitcase full of my things)

Fear returns.
What neighborhood is this?
Never thought love would shut me out;
(To whose abode am I trying to gain entry?)

Touch NOTHING!
Bomb squad and forensics will be here to investigate the scene:

My heart in the yard,
and you hiding from my terror.

once again

MARK REMAINED IN MERCY HOSPITAL for the requisite seventy-two-hour hold. Then he stayed a few additional days when Michelle noticed he was not getting better. Mark had voluntarily taken a drug test that showed no illegal substances. The attending physician told Michelle, "The bipolar illness seems to have crashed through Mark's present medication." The doctor then changed Mark's prescriptions, giving him Risperdal, an antipsychotic medication, as well as an increased dosage of Depakote. Within one week, Mark began to respond to the changes and returned home. During his recovery period, he resumed his writing:

> *The ghost pain of amputated fear*
> *is all that's left.*
> *I am startled,*
> > *now and then,*
> *by nothing.*

We were not expecting Mark to bounce back immediately once he was released from the hospital. He was exhausted from his long ordeal, and he was still somewhat uncomfortable in his familiar surroundings at home. "Is it OK if I use the couch to take a nap, Michelle?" he asked politely. He slept most of the day. Mark's doctor predicted a recovery period of several months and recommended bed rest and minimal stress so that Mark could regain his balance. Dexter, his manager at the store, gave Mark several days at home "to get himself together" before returning to his full-time employment. He did not ask Mark for details. Looking back on it, I realize that Dexter had always been quietly in

Mark's corner. When he thought Mark was being testy at work, he suggested that Mark take a day off. We were so grateful for his understanding.

Michelle's mother traveled from New England to Atlanta to help with the kids. Houston and I supported Mark and Michelle as best we could with daily phone calls. We knew from past episodes that our presence was not wanted in Atlanta. At the end of her first day in their home, Michelle's mother gently reported to us over the telephone, "Well, he's not all the way back. But every now and then I can see 'our Mark' in there. I think he's slowly getting better. It's really so sad."

Every day, Michelle called us in Durham and kept us abreast of Mark's progress. "It really gets me down when he bounces back and forth between being sad and being too happy," Michelle reported. As Easter approached, Michelle's mother prepared to return home. With news of her impending departure, Houston and I thought of visiting. We knew Michelle could use the help. We were nervous since this would be the first time in two years we had planned a visit while Mark was still ill.

When we arrived, the first sight of Mark warmed me, and I realized how much I missed him. I hugged him hello as long as I could. He looked rosy in the face, but his movements were slow. Eventually, he broke into a smile and invited us inside. During our first evening, Mark helped readily with the household chores. He pitched in with dinner preparations and later mopped up an accidental spill in the kitchen. I was so proud of him. An hour later, his stamina gave out, and he snapped an answer at Michelle when she simply asked, "What are you doing, Mark?" She saw me flinch at Mark's curt response and quickly replied, "It's OK, Mom. He doesn't mean anything by it. He just gets touchy when he's not well."

The next evening as we left the dinner table, I asked, "Can I help in here with the dishes?"

"Since when did you ever like doing the dishes?" Mark responded sharply. I disregarded his comment and proceeded to scrape the plates. I knew then that I needed to make my presence scarce during the next few days.

On Easter Sunday morning, our last full day in Atlanta, everyone moved along expeditiously as we dressed for church services. We all settled into the car, and, as we drove, Mark began to quarrel sotto voce with Michelle about directions to the church. They had decided to attend a different church for Easter Mass. Sitting in the backseat, I could feel the tension building. Jack kept his nose close to his Game Boy, and Houston and I pretended to comment on the passing neighborhoods.

By the time we got to church, everyone was a bit jumpy. There were only a few spaces left, so Houston and I sat separately from Mark, Michelle, and the children and did not see the encounter Mark had with a parishioner. After church, Michelle edged up to me and said tightly, "Mark's not happy. He thinks I'm angry with him because he made a scene in church." She explained that Mark had become hostile with the man seated behind them when he tried to play peekaboo with Eric. With his special brand of antagonism, Mark turned and glared at the man. Michelle was deeply embarrassed.

"He had no business staring at my baby," Mark declared. We drove home in silence.

Once home, we all pitched in to arrange the Easter dinner Michelle had prepared so meticulously: ham with pineapple glaze and the accompanying side dishes of mashed potatoes, green beans, and apples. When Michelle's sister arrived with her two children, Michelle gave them all Easter baskets with jellybeans and chocolates. Houston tried to cheer up the atmosphere by playing "red light, green light" with Jack and the kids. Mark remained sullen during dinner, and we all tried to avoid his stare. He rudely pushed food around his plate, and just before dessert, he bolted from the table. No one asked his whereabouts. The next day, Houston and I left for home. I felt as if I had been holding my breath for two days straight.

In Durham, I continued to worry about what was happening in Atlanta. When we left, Mark was moody and hostile. The children were exhibiting signs of stress. Michelle carried the baby constantly, and each time she put him down, he cried. Jack was quiet and watchful. Houston and I felt hopeless. We did not know how else to support Mark and his family. We had tried visiting, sending money, and paying for extra child care. These strategies had helped, but only superficially. My eyes filled with tears at the oddest times, and I avoided my colleagues at work. I was so emotionally fraught one day that I started to cry when one of my students told me she had received an unexpected service award.

Houston was better at hiding his frustration. He kept busy with work at school and managed to distract himself. When he finished with his university business, he turned to the minutia of rechecking monthly bills at home, "just to be sure they're up to date," he said. He already knew most of them were being deducted automatically because he had set up the accounts. Keeping his emotions at bay, Houston told me he felt as if our lives were unraveling. Our financial situation was strained. Nevertheless, we continued to help Mark and Michelle each time they had a household emergency. A month earlier, their house had needed repair; the basement took in water whenever there was a hard rain. Silently, I worried, *Will this never end?* I despaired for Mark, Michelle, and their family.

Houston and I made an appointment with our North Carolina therapist, Dr. M., who had talked us through some of Mark's previous difficulties. At our first session, Dr. M. suggested that Houston and I take a weekend trip away to relax and gather our thoughts. We followed her suggestion and went to New York, our favorite nearby city. The first morning there, about nine o'clock, I heard the hotel housekeeper tap on the door and ask to make up our room. I said, "No, thanks," and rolled over to sleep another hour. When we both awakened, I ordered room service. It was after one o'clock when we finally descended to the lobby. New York City awaited us, but our pace was necessarily slow.

When we returned to North Carolina, we saw Dr. M. and told her about our last visit to see Mark and Michelle in Atlanta. With her support, once again, we tried to accept the fact that we could not save Mark. Our role was to intervene only if asked. We hoped that Mark and Michelle would decide how to protect their children during their intermittent periods of bipolar distress. They were also experiencing money problems and had almost no time alone together. I thought they needed personal support as a couple. Dr. M. recommended that they discover Atlanta support systems and make use of them. She challenged me to let Mark and Michelle find their own way. She hoped Houston and I would focus on our own life together.

reflections on writing

DURING THIS PERIOD, I BEGAN to keep a journal in which I recorded my thoughts about Mark's bipolar disorder. I also continued researching the illness. This helped me focus on something productive, a necessary respite from thinking only about Mark. I especially appreciated Kay Redfield Jamison's book, *An Unquiet Mind*; it heightened my understanding of Mark's illness. While reading Jamison's account of her own bipolar disorder, I realized that what was happening to Mark was not his fault. Although this should have been an obvious realization after the many crises we had encountered, I needed a degree of separation from my own troubles to assimilate it. This was a turning point for me. Jamison's vividly descriptive language about her bipolar disorder allowed me to experience someone else's struggles. The episodes she recounted were so similar to Mark's that my empathy for him deepened. As I continued to read, my anger and sadness became less acute. I realized I wanted to write Mark's story. The literature on bipolar disorder, at that time, was almost entirely by and about white people.

In my research on bipolar disorder, I plunged into a sea of definitions that I previously thought I understood. *Mania* is an abnormal and dramatic upswing in mood or a mental disorder characterized by intense excitement and, sometimes, violent behavior. *Hypomania* is a less severe form of mania, characterized by a great sense of well-being in the person who experiences it. I was learning to differentiate the terms by watching my own son. When I told Houston about my prospective writing project, he listened and quietly reminded me that I already had a full-time teaching position. "Many people teach and write at the same time. The focus will give me purpose," I told him. He realized my determination and offered his support.

I retreated into the private space of writing and saw from a distance that Mark and Michelle were doing better. On the home front, they were successfully working out a schedule in which Michelle cared for Jack and their new baby while Mark worked at his retail job. As the doctor had suggested, Michelle weaned the baby to a bottle formula and resumed her medication therapy. She joined an organized mothers' group and spent time with them at the nearby playground and began to swap babysitting with other mothers in her group. When I spoke with Michelle, she sounded strong and resolute. She told me excitedly that Mark had joined a gym, and they had recently enrolled in couples' therapy to find ways to support each other. Houston and I were so relieved to hear about their resolutions. They were pleased that their newborn, Eric, was sleeping through the night. Mark sent me the most affectionate note by e-mail: "Love you, Mommo. Thanks a lot. Keep writing."

About a year after I started writing, I considered the idea of weaving some of Mark's poetry and prose throughout my manuscript. I thought that having Mark's words alongside mine might help readers understand how Mark felt when he was ill and show how his illness impacted his life. I continuously reread poems, trying to fathom the two Marks who seemed to inhabit his writing: one well and the other manic, edgy, and, at times, delusional. I realized that, in my early reading, some of his poetic references had escaped me. For example, in the following poem, "After the Fall," I came to grasp the multiple meanings of "snow" and "fall":

A naked bulb
illuminates these daffodil walls,
like flash of a camera
suspended in time.

Sound, here, is paralyzed,
except for the thud of an occasional bee
flying into screen of an open window.
All else has disappeared
into the vacuum of quieted thoughts
And hushed voices.

Smell of fresh paint reaches nostrils
no longer outlined in snow.
It is the unfamiliar scent
of blooming dreams
and a loyal spring
that,
like a soul mate,
rains love
forever.

This poem took on new meaning for me after I remembered Mark's admission to a counselor that he had used cocaine. How had I forgotten this?

I called Mark to explain my idea for incorporating his writing in my project, and I asked his permission. He answered reluctantly, "I'm not sure, Mom. I thought one day I might publish some of my poems myself."

I understood Mark's reservation, and I let the subject drop temporarily. I continued to write and research bipolar disorder. I also continued reading Mark's poetry and prose. During his childhood and young-adult years, Mark and I had always enjoyed talking to each other, in person and on paper. I realized that Mark's illness had interrupted this aspect of our relationship.

As a child, Mark loved to write, and I enjoyed reading whatever he shared. One day, with a serious, ten-year-old's stare, he asked me, "Mom, why do you always say you like my poems?"

"Well, in that poem you just gave me, I like the way you describe the trees. It makes me see them," I told him.

When he was in fifth grade, Mark brought home a short story written in class, "Dudley Crenshaw, the Nobody." In the story, Dudley, younger than Mark at the time, was sad because his class-mates shamelessly teased him for being a nerd and reading all the time. By the end of the story, Dudley had gained recognition from his schoolmates. Houston and I were so fond of the story that we asked Mark to read it for his grandparents when they came to visit. I pulled dining room chairs up to the fireplace in the living room and called it a story reading. Our small family audience applauded vigorously at the end of Mark's reading.

I recently asked Mark if he remembered the story. He imme-diately laughed and responded, "Oh, yeah. I remember Dudley." I marveled that he had not forgotten.

"I got a lot of praise for that short story," he said. "My teacher loved it, too. I think I still have it somewhere in one of my school boxes." At the time, neither Houston nor I considered that Dudley might have been Mark in disguise.

Mark continued to write stories, and gradually he began to write poetry. His early verse was youthful, giving no hint of the mature poet he would become. Nonetheless, Mark knew that I enjoyed reading every line. I loved his joy in translating emotions into words. When I recently asked Mark why he had shared his poetry with me, even later when he was ill and in jail, he paused and then responded, "I'm not sure. I never asked myself that question. You know, I guess I just trusted you with that part of me."

After our traumatic home invasion in 1981, when he was ten, Mark wrote this piece:

When Mom is gone nothing is right and everything is wrong,
A joke is not a joke, and the birds don't sing their song.
When Mom is gone school is not as fun as it used to be,

And a tree is just a tree.
When Mom is gone nothing is as it used to be.
Snow is just snow, and rain is just rain.
But if Mom came back,
a joke would be funny, school would be fun,
the rain would be as nice as gold,
the snow would sparkle clear against the sun,
and the birds would sing their song.
But nothing is the way it used to be when Mom is gone.

Sometime during junior high school, Mark stopped giving me poetry. His themes turned to romance, and I suspected then that his poems were finding more age-specific recipients. Instead of giving me poetry, he asked me to read drafts of his essays for history or English and to catch grammatical mistakes and punctuation errors. In high school, he started again to share his writing with me. When I recently asked Mark if he had kept any of his high school poetry, he responded, "I'm not sure, but I'll give a look in my file." Within a few days, he sent several poems. I had no idea he had saved so many. Here is one of my favorites:

Manchester Lane

I was so small,
Almost swallowed by the half-finished basement
Of my grandparents' home
While, above, adults sang
Barely identifiable lyrics
To ancient, yet unheard songs.

The chest that sat against a corner,
Beside a painting of some distant place
I now believe was Paris,
Became my shelter

As I marched to and from those dust-
laden antiques, exploring.

Once a year the family would descend,
Scrap-paper bets in hand,
And sit atop tables and frayed arm chairs
To watch The Derby.
I won once and have never forgotten the yellow-
tinted 19 inch in a back room
Of that place.

Christmas
Was always a treat.
When I was nine,
I recorded the morning's gift giving
But lost the tape.
Decembers were always for family,
Carols with Johnny Mathis
And German chocolate cake.
Now, they carry death
On snow burdened wings . . .
Chilling joys at remembering how the month
Saw my grandfather off,
And the tired face of his wife
As she spoke painfully of selling the house.

We drove by last year
And smiling imaginations beheld
The rose beds –
Now gone,
Still in vibrant bloom.

When I first read this poem, it brought me immediate delight.
I thought of Houston's father making roaring fires in the fireplace

and the smell of German chocolate cake as only Houston's mother could make it. Their chest of drawers now belongs to me. It contains Mark's grandmother's quilts and stands in the guest bedroom of our present home. I remembered the Kentucky Derby ritual that Houston's father insisted we follow each year. He had us choose our favorite Derby horse and write its number on a slip of paper. I can still feel the excited tension in our group as we watched the horses race around the track, and we all waited eagerly to see whose horse would win. I remember the year that Mark's horse won and the look of pride on his face when he collected our total pool of fifteen dollars. It was a bleak winter when my father-in-law died. Mark's poem captures it all.

Much later, after Mark left graduate school and was recovering from a major bipolar episode, he had difficulty reading and writing. His attention span was short, and he began to write in cryptic, sometimes haiku-like, verse. He sent me a few pieces from this period. In one entry, he wrote simply:

We paint our own stories. Mine were written in blood diluted with tears,
a red ellipsis on the end . . .

Anything longer than a short string of words frustrated him. Mark said he wrote simple lines because "that's as much as I could think. And it was like my eyesight was failing."

Two years later, just prior to another episode, the cadence of Mark's poetry shifted yet again. In the following excerpt from one of his poems, I was able to sense his hypomania, an on-the-brink-of-mania rhythm:

(A Manic Freedom)
(Let's just throw a couple of special effects in there for the kids to love on until we find a solution) to the quintessential problem that is:

is that, the streets are most definitely watching us
clocking us
dropping us on our asses
and there is no room to bounce
before you
or one
is caught
in a conundrum
that is paradoxical
to any way that you thought you had a God-given right to feel
and so u feel cheated
and defeated
like a panther without his meat, or
hurt
and you don't even anymore know
how
or not how
to feel
or fear
or even resort to drinking beer
not malt though,
because it's "rotgut," yr grandmomma said . . .

so anyway,

I was baffled when I first read this poem and had to read it several times. Gradually, I sensed the hip-hop rhythm of his pen, and I understood the meaning of his words: "the streets are most definitely watching us / clocking us." The words reminded me of the moment he telephoned from the streets of Los Angeles, pleading, "Mom, help me. They're watching me." Mark forgets very little. Writing is his way of recording the experiences of his world.

When Mark came to visit us in North Carolina for a weekend in 1997 on a pass from Skyland, he brought poetry with him and asked if he could share some of it. When we settled in to listen to his new poems, I was surprised that most of them did not engage me. I could not figure out why. As the three of us sat in the living room eating popcorn, Mark said, "Can you believe I'm sitting here visiting you on a 'weekend pass' from a mental hospital?" Even while Mark was in recovery, his sense of humor reigned. Afterward, I realized what was missing for me in Mark's new poems. They lacked the risk taking of some of his older writing. Mark agreed. "You're right, Mom. I think I was scared, giving up my old life, but I had to keep writing."

The following year, Mark completed his rehabilitation. During that same period, he and Michelle got married. My writing was proceeding well, and I had several polished sections of my work in progress. I asked Mark once again if I could use some of his writing in my manuscript. "When I use your writing next to mine, it's like music," I told him. He smiled.

"Don't give me an answer yet," I said. "I'm further along with the manuscript now, so I'll send you a couple of segments to read. See what you think." I suggested that he discuss the sections with Michelle.

After two months, Mark called to say he and Michelle had finished reading: "It's hard stuff to read, Mom. I had no idea I was going to like it so much. Yes, you have my permission to use my writing. Use whatever you want!" I was surprised and happy. He told me that he and Michelle had talked long into the night about the writing I sent them. They decided that our family narrative might help others struggling with bipolar disorder.

atlanta book trip

IN LATE JUNE 2006, I made arrangements to go to Atlanta. I decided to travel alone so that Mark, Michelle, and I could read through the drafted pages I had sent. "You can make comments and tell me what you don't like," I told them. Michelle was in the final months of her pregnancy with their second son. She and Mark had decided already that his name would be Carter. In spite of their imminent event, they both welcomed my visit. I hoped to squeeze in some playtime with little Eric and give Jack some special attention while I was there. I knew that on my next visit, there would be three grandsons to capture my attention.

My first morning in Atlanta, Mark interrupted the "eensy, weensy spider song" that Jack and I were singing to Eric. Mark said, "We'll take a few hours this evening to go over the book. Is that OK, Mom?" I agreed.

After we had dinner together and Mark and Michelle read stories to the children, the three of us got comfortable on the living room sofa with manuscript pages in hand. Taking the lead, Mark intoned, "OK. Let's begin. Page one." As I sat there, following along and answering their questions, I smiled to myself. Mark had called my project "the book."

At one point, Mark took issue with my casual assertion in the draft that his poetry and prose had been "originally taken from his journal while in jail." He firmly corrected me: "Mom, you just don't understand. There was no way I could keep a journal in jail. I was not even allowed to keep a pen and paper!"

Incredulous, I asked, "Why not? What in the world could you do with a pen and paper except write?"

In my mind's eye, I had imagined Mark in jail, gaining solace from his writing. That belief had comforted me. But Mark was shaking his head and told me, "I did the writing in my journal after I got out of jail. My head was so messed up, I'm not sure I could have written anything while I was there."

Witnessing my look of bafflement, Mark held up one finger and abruptly left the room. For a moment, I thought I had offended him, but he quickly returned. Between his thumb and forefinger he held a small, tightly folded square of paper. He slowly unfolded the thin, dingy paper, saying, "This is what I mean, Mom."

He talked as he examined the paper, as if it was his first time seeing it. "If you wanted paper, you had to use whatever was available," he explained. "This one guy got to have a Bible for his good behavior, and he tore a sheet from the front of it and gave it to me to write on. I already had a small piece of pencil hidden away."

The room got quiet. Mark handed me the paper.

Gingerly, I took the delicate sheet. In between the lines of typeface that read "The Holy Bible, Old and New Testaments," Mark had copied a psalm, "because it spoke to me." Sure enough, I saw Mark's precise writing in tiny block print, in the corners, around the margins, in between the lettering: "Out of the depths I cry to You, O Lord / O Lord, hear my voice." The poetry is not even his own, I thought.

As I stood there holding the onionskin paper, not knowing what to say, Mark spoke up, "I sneaked that paper out with me when I was released. I keep it because it reminds me of my freedom."

We did not finish the manuscript pages that night. "It's OK," Michelle chimed in. "We can start tomorrow, early, when we get up. I'm sure we can finish by dinnertime."

The next day, we talked about Mark's descriptions of jail and the particular anecdotes I had chosen to use in the manuscript.

Some details were a surprise to me. In his journal during that period, he had written:

On the outside, I hardly ever picked up a Bible during the course of an average day. In here, I read a portion of the Bible daily—I took notes, even. I wrote my favorite passages from Psalms, Proverbs, the Book of John. I read as if I'm studying for a final exam. I assure God I will never pick up a drug again if only He will help me out of my present predicament. I repeat The Lord's Prayer, The Hail Mary, and The Act of Contrition, the prayer for forgiveness of one's sins. I say the rosary without the beads.

As I reread portions of the manuscript, I lost all track of time. Suddenly, it was one o'clock in the morning. Without disagreement, the three of us had dissected Mark's poetry and prose and decided where it should be placed in the one hundred pages we had all been examining. There was nothing in it that Michelle did not already know. She and Mark had talked about every line and every situation. Their protection of each other sobered me. Michelle watched Mark's reaction to everything I said, and he watched her as she talked. I was comforted to know that our son had such a supportive partner. In the end, I was not just writing about Mark's struggles. I was writing about the two of them.

Two days later, I returned home. I promised to send more pages just as soon as I had them.

epilogue

RECENTLY, MARK SAID TO ME, "You know, if I had not gotten sick and gone to Skyland Trail, I would never have met Michelle. She is everything to me." Had Mark not been diagnosed with bipolar disorder, I would never have written this book. I would not be on the Skyland Trail board of directors. I would not have gained the compassion and strength I now have from traveling this particular road. When I remember my lack of knowledge about mental illness years ago, I realize that my son's terrifying call for help was a moment of transformation in my life. I am well aware that I have been blessed with emotional and financial resources to support an adult son with a disability. I know that my family is extremely fortunate in this regard.

Houston and I worry about the future. We talk endlessly about who will love and take care of our children when we are no longer around. We think of mortality more than we ever did in the past. One of my personal fears is the thought of Mark having to manage his illness without Houston or me there to offer backup support. My love for Mark is profound. I am proud of his gifts and his fortitude. I feel as if we have gotten Mark to the top of an enormous mountain, and now we ask ourselves, "Who will make the journey with him from here?" We hope that Mark and Michelle will continue to find people who can provide the medical support they sometimes need.

The last decade and a half has taught me that living with bipolar disorder is not about assessing progress. Rather, it is about perseverance. Mark has learned to live with his illness as best he can. Sometimes, he is well enough to work and to care for his family without stress. Most of the time, he is able to cheer from the sidelines at Jack's football games. On occasion, he arranges beach holidays for the family. At other times, Mark's bipolar disorder takes over and requires him to get extra rest, try a different medication, or even endure hospitalization. I know there is no cure for our son's illness.

I take nothing for granted. Neither does Mark.

The rain
taps Morse code rhythms on my roof.
I decipher its inner-meaning
as if sifting color from silence.
It is the sound of shattered dreams mending;
an end to the false hope of rainbows.

acknowledgments

WRITING IS PLEASURABLE BUT NEVER without anxiety. When the topic is mental illness and one's son, days of composition become long and sometimes excruciating. Nights are often wakeful. Many people have made the writing process less onerous. You will recognize yourself by direct reference or by discreet pseudonym. You are all embedded in the pages of *This Fragile Life*. If by chance you are missing, please know your face will come to me in the night, and I will cringe at my oversight. My and Mark's gratitude for your presence and support suffuses every page of this book. You are now family. Thank you, Wanda. Thank you, Tesse.

Thank you, Philadelphia, through the University of Pennsylvania and the Germantown Friends School, for allowing us to make mistakes and for nurturing us as we made them. We learned so very much from you and your friendships. Thank you, Kay Redfield Jamison, for *An Unquiet Mind*, a book that empowered me to begin my journey with Mark.

Thank you, colleagues and friends at Duke University and in Durham. You were the first to hear about my intended project on bipolar disorder. Your reading of initial pages and suggestions for the inclusion of particular anecdotes and topics were much appreciated. You are staff, faculty, colleagues, Family-to-Family friends of NAMI (National Alliance on Mental Illness), and family psychotherapists. Thank you, Anne Mulkern, MD, Maureen Quilligan and Michael Malone, Priscilla Wald and Joe Donahue, Cathy Davidson and Ken Wissoker, Rick Powell and C. T. Woods Powell, Marianna and Stuart Torgovnick, Lincoln Hancock, and others. Many of you gave Houston and me sustenance when we had nowhere else to turn.

Many of you with whom I spoke in Durham were mental health consumers who urged me to write the story of my son. You know who you are, and I thank you for your inspiring stories. Thank you for not allowing me to turn back.

Chicago friends (Voices and Faces) and colleague-friends at the University of Illinois at Chicago, thank you for listening to my early ideas for the manuscript and for carrying me through Mark's episodes during that period. As I think back to 2003, I remember your acts of extreme kindness and patience. You have my sincere gratitude: Mary Beth Rose, Julia and Alan Thomas, Jane Tompkins and Stanley Fish, Anne Ream, Clifton Spargo, Patsy Evans and Jamie Kalven, Beth Richie, Sharon Holland and Jennifer Brody, Walter Benn Michaels and Jennifer Ashton, Gerald Graff and Cathy Birkenstein-Graff, Lisa Freeman, Lennard Davis, Helen Jun, Michael and Roslyn Lieb.

Now, as I complete my book at Vanderbilt University, a similar kindness abounds. Mona Frederick, Julia Fesmire, Rory Dicker, Monica Casper, Barbara Kaeser, Julie Sandine, Kitti Wirtz, Nora Spencer, Kacy Silverstein, Kenneth Robinson, Amy Hodges-Hamilton and Forest Hamilton, Frank Dobson, Jeff King, Natalie Baggett, Hortense Spillers and Howard Romaine, Alice Randall and David Ewing, Stan and Alena Thangaraj, Bonnie Dow and John Sloop, Carolyn Dever, Nick Zeppos and Lydia Howarth, Richard and Sheila McCarty, Dana Nelson and Tom Dillehay, Jay and Ellen Clayton, Mark Schoenfield: Thank you for your onward cheering and for allowing me space and time to write. Thank you for taking up the slack when I needed time away from the office. You have been enduring in your caring.

A very special thank you goes to my Vanderbilt colleagues and friends in the Trauma Research Fellows group of the Robert Penn

Warren Center at Vanderbilt University during 2008 and 2009: Vivien Fryd (our fearsome leader), Laura Carpenter, Linda Manning, Kate Daniels, Jon Ebert, Christina Karageorgou-Bastea, Maurice Stevens, and Claire Sisco King. Our year of research, writing, and sharing was undeniably important to my book. Your insights and our conversations were supportive and encouraging. You gave me the audacity I needed to approach mental illness and the family trauma I was living.

Our longtime family physicians and friends came to our aid each and every time we called: Robert Smith, MD, Geraldine De Paula, MD, and Steven Rolfe, MD; Arnold Rampersad and Marvina White; Valerie Smith; Ellen and Bill Dohmen; Bessie Jordan and Sandy Byrd; Betty-Ann Workman and family; Bettina Yaffe and Gino Segré; Nancy Venable Raine and Steve Stevick; Beverly and Stuart Gerber; Jim Nash and Teri Gatto Nash; Emy Halpert; Gregory Alexander; Aileen Christianson; Marjorie Levinson and Richard Harris; Gary and Rinna Gack; Bill James and family; Bob Smith and Lorene Cary; Patricia LeBon-Herb and Guntram Herb; Tama and Paul Hampton; Flora and Mertol "Mike" Jackson; Heather Russell; Jewell Parker Rhodes and family. Some of you have been with us since Mark's birth, and others have joined us along the way. We would not be standing at this time, in this moment, had it not been for your caring ministrations. I send profound gratitude.

My family has been with me through the difficulties of writing this book and Mark's ongoing illness. Appreciation goes, especially, to my brother and friend, Joseph Carlyle Pierce Jr. and his wife, Sue Ahearn; my brother-in-law John Baker (in memoriam) and his wife, Eleanor. Joe, you have been unwavering in your support, and you have been a splendid, caring uncle to Mark. I send big hugs to my niece, Sonya, and my nephews, Mike and Ivan, Gregory and Benjamin. The same affection I extend to my aunts, Gwendolyn, Amy, and Mildred and to my cousins and friends, Reggie, Karen,

Lori, Sharon, Gerald, and Toni. Our deceased parents, Houston Sr., Viola Smith Baker, Joseph Sr., and Weslyne Carroll Pierce were extraordinary mentors. In our adulthood, they were nurturing and steadfast friends. We admire their love for their grandson.

I extend gratitude to Mark West and the board, staff, physicians, and therapists at Skyland Trail. Their support, expertise, and caring brought Mark back to us. Beth Finnerty deserves signal praise. More than once, she went beyond the call of duty. Thank you to MARR, Doug Brush and staff; I offer my gratitude to Program SAFE in Atlanta, for letting Mark rest at their doors while he waited for Skyland.

Thanks to my agent, Jane Dystel, who is always in my corner. Thank you, Jane, for finding a home for my manuscript, *This Fragile Life*. Thanks also to agents Stephanie DeVita and Rachel Stout of Dystel and Goderich Literary Management. You have been generous, professional, and caring throughout the entire process of my book's gestation. Thank you to Sue Betz, my brilliant editor and advocate at Lawrence Hill Books/Chicago Review Press. Thank you, Sue, for liking and accepting my work. Thanks also to the copyeditors and design stars at Chicago Review Press whom I have never met.

Church has been essential to my journey. The pastor and community of Immaculate Conception Church in Durham, North Carolina, supported us through difficult moments of Mark's illness. The St. Matthew's Church community was empathetic as well. As current members of St. Ann's parish in Nashville, Tennessee, we have found another nurturing community. In particular, thank you, Father Philip Breen, for reminding us to "keep on keeping on."

I offer profound gratitude to Melissa Solomon, who was my research assistant when I began. Melissa agreed to stay on when I left North Carolina for Tennessee. She became my perceptive editor, wise consultant, and the first reader of many drafts. She has been my fantastic cheering squad. Thank you, Melissa! Your loyalty is unsurpassed.

Family is what I chose to write about. I want our grandchildren to know the courage of their father and their mother. Their parents' love made this book possible, and now their extended love for their children enables them to commit to wellness. The story of Mark and Michelle is a gift whose passage, I hope, will offer encouragement to others who face the challenges of mental illness.

Thank you, Michelle, for your trust.

Thank you, Mark, for giving permission for your words and your life to become public. Your courage instructs and nurtures my life every hour of every day.

Thank you, Houston, for your love and partnership. I would not have wanted to make this journey with anyone else.

bibliography/resources

Fiction

Coleman, Carter. *Cage's Bend*. New York: Warner Books, 2005.

Exley, Frederick. *A Fan's Notes*. New York: Random House, 1968.

Fromm, Pete. *How All This Started*. New York: Picador, 2000.

Gibbons, Kaye. *Sights Unseen*. New York: G. P. Putnam's Sons, 1995.

Plath, Sylvia. *The Bell Jar*. New York: Harper and Row, 1971.

Nonfiction and Memoirs

Barber, Charles. *Songs from the Black Chair: A Memoir of Mental Interiors*. Lincoln: University of Nebraska Press, 2005.

Behrman, Andy. *Electroboy: A Memoir of Mania*. New York: Random House, 2002.

Cheney, Terri. *Manic: A Memoir*. New York: HarperCollins, 2008.

Duke, Patty, and Gloria Hochman. *A Brilliant Madness: Living with Manic-Depressive Illness*. New York: Bantam Books, 1992.

Early, Pete. *Crazy: A Father's Search Through America's Mental Health Madness*. New York: G. P. Putnam's Sons, 2006.

Hinshaw, Stephen P. *The Years of Silence Are Past: My Father's Life with Bipolar Disorder*. New York: Cambridge University Press, 2002.

Jamison, Kay Redfield. *An Unquiet Mind: A Memoir of Moods and Madness*. New York: Alfred A. Knopf, 1995.

——. *Night Falls Fast: Understanding Suicide*. New York: Alfred A. Knopf, 1999.

Karr, Mary. *The Liar's Club: A Memoir*. New York: Penguin, 1995.

Kaysen, Susanna. *Girl, Interrupted*. New York: Turtle Bay Books, 1993.

Manning, Martha. *Undercurrents: A Life Beneath the Surface*. New York: HarperCollins, 1994.

Nasar, Sylvia. *A Beautiful Mind: The Life of Mathematical Genius and Nobel Laureate John Nash*. New York: Simon & Schuster, 1998.

O'Brien, Sharon. *The Family Silver: A Memoir of Depression and Inheritance*. Chicago: University of Chicago Press, 2004.

Raeburn, Paul. *Acquainted with the Night: A Parent's Quest to Understand Depression and Bipolar Disorder in His Children*. New York: Broadway Books, 2004.

Saks, Elyn R. *The Center Cannot Hold: My Journey Through Madness*. New York: Hyperion, 2007.

Simon, Lizzie. *Detour: My Bipolar Road Trip in 4-D*. New York: Atria Books, 2002.

Slater, Lauren. *Welcome to My Country: A Therapist's Memoir of Madness*. New York: Anchor Books, 1996.

Steel, Danielle. *His Bright Light: The Story of Nick Traina*. New York: Delacorte Press, 1998.

Styron, William. *Darkness Visible: A Memoir of Madness*. New York: Random House, 1990.

Medically Based Sources

American Psychiatric Association. *Diagnostic and Statistical Manual of Mental Disorders,* 4th ed. Washington, DC: American Psychiatric Association, 1994.

Andreasen, Nancy C., MD, PhD. *The Broken Brain: The Biological Revolution in Psychiatry.* New York: Harper and Row, 1984.

Beutler, Larry E., and Mary L. Malik. *Rethinking the DSM: A Psychological Perspective.* Washington, DC: American Psychological Association, 2002.

Breggin, Peter R., MD, and David Cohen, PhD. *Your Drug May Be Your Problem: How and Why to Stop Taking Psychiatric Drugs.* New York: Perseus Books, 1999.

Maj, Mario, Hagop S. Akiskal, Juan Jose Lopez-Ibor Jr., and Norman Sartorius, eds. *Bipolar Disorder.* West Sussex, UK: John Wiley and Sons, 2002.

Marneros, Andreas, and Jules Angst. *Bipolar Disorders: 100 Years after Manic-Depressive Insanity.* Boston: Kluwer Academic Publishers, 2000.

Marohn, Stephanie. *The Natural Medicine Guide to Bipolar Disorder.* Charlottesville, VA: Hampton Roads Publishing, 2003.

Martin, Emily. *Bipolar Expeditions: Mania and Depression in American Culture.* Princeton, NJ: Princeton University Press, 2007.

Parker, Gordon. *Bipolar II Disorder: Modelling, Measuring and Managing.* Cambridge, UK: Cambridge University Press, 2008.

Ratey, John J., MD. *Mental Retardation: Developing Pharmacotherapies.* Washington, DC: American Psychiatric Press, 1991.

Shorter, Edward. *A History of Psychiatry: From the Era of the Asylum to the Age of Prozac*. New York: John Wiley and Sons, 1997.

Whybrow, Peter C., MD. *A Mood Apart: Depression, Mania, and Other Afflictions of the Self*. New York: HarperCollins, 1997.

Wolpert, Edward A., ed. *Manic-Depressive Illness: History of a Syndrome*. New York: International Universities Press, 1977.

Self-Help

Fast, Julie A., and John A. Preston, PsyD. *Loving Someone with Bipolar Disorder: Understanding and Helping Your Partner*. Oakland, CA: New Harbinger Publications, 2004.

Fawcett, Jan, MD, Bernard Golden, PhD, and Nancy Rosenfeld. *New Hope for People with Bipolar Disorder*. New York: Three Rivers Press, 2000.

Fink, Candida, MD, and Joseph Kraynak. *Bipolar Disorder for Dummies*. Hoboken, NJ: Wiley Publishing, 2005.

Hales, Dianne, and Robert E. Hales, MD. *Caring for the Mind: The Comprehensive Guide to Mental Health*. New York: Bantam, 2005.

Jamieson, Patrick E. *Mind Race: A Firsthand Account of One Teenager's Experience with Bipolar Disorder*. New York: Oxford University Press, 2006.

Karp, David A. *The Burden of Sympathy: How Families Cope with Mental Illness*. New York: Oxford University Press, 2001.

Koplewicz, Harold S., MD. *It's Nobody's Fault: New Hope and Help for Difficult Children*. New York: Three Rivers Press, 1996.

Miklowitz, David J., PhD. *The Bipolar Disorder Survival Guide: What You and Your Family Need to Know*. New York: Guilford Press, 2002.

Mondimore, Francis Mark, MD. *Bipolar Disorder: A Guide for Patients and Families*. Baltimore: Johns Hopkins University Press, 1999.

Mountain, Jane, MD. *Bipolar Disorder: Insights for Recovery*. Denver: Chapter One Press, 2003.

Papolos, Demitri, and Janice Papolos. *The Bipolar Child: The Definitive and Reassuring Guide to Childhood's Most Misunderstood Disorder*. New York: Broadway Books, 1999.

Secunda, Victoria. *When Madness Comes Home: Help and Hope for the Children, Siblings, and Partners of the Mentally Ill*. New York: Hyperion, 1997.

Solomon, Andrew. *The Noonday Demon: An Atlas of Depression*. New York: Scribner, 2001.

Spickard, Anderson, Jr., MD, and Barbara R. Thompson. *Dying for a Drink: What You and Your Family Should Know About Alcoholism*. Nashville: Thomas Nelson, 2005.

Torrey, E. Fuller, MD. *Out of the Shadows: Confronting America's Mental Illness Crisis*. New York: John Wiley and Sons, 1997.

———. *Surviving Manic Depression: A Manual on Bipolar Disorder for Patients, Families, and Providers*. New York: Basic Books, 2005.

Cultural Perspectives on Mental Illness

Davis, Mike. *City of Quartz: Excavating the Future in Los Angeles*. London: Verso, 1990.

Foucault, Michel. *Madness and Civilization: A History of Insanity in the Age of Reason.* New York: Random House, 1965.

———. *The Birth of the Clinic: An Archaeology of Medical Perception.* New York: Pantheon Books, 1973.

———. *Mental Illness and Psychology.* New York: Harper and Row, 1976.

Grob, Gerald N. *Mental Illness and American Society, 1875–1940.* Princeton, NJ: Princeton University Press, 1983.

Jamison, Kay Redfield. *Touched with Fire: Manic-Depressive Illness and the Artistic Temperament.* New York: Knopf, 1999.

Luhrmann, T. M. *Of Two Minds: An Anthropologist Looks at American Psychiatry.* New York: Vintage Books, 2001.

Rathbone, Cristina. *A World Apart: Women, Prison, and Life Behind Bars.* New York: Random House, 2002.

Scarry, Elaine. *The Body in Pain: The Making and Unmaking of the World.* New York: Oxford University Press, 1985.

Sontag, Susan. *Illness as Metaphor.* New York: Vintage Books, 1977.

African Americans and Mental Illness

Bell, Carl C., MD. *The Sanity of Survival: Reflections on Community Mental Health and Wellness.* Chicago: Third World Press, 2004.

Billingsley, Andrew. *Climbing Jacob's Ladder: The Enduring Legacy of African-American Families.* New York: Simon & Schuster, 1992.

Campbell, Bebe Moore. *72 Hour Hold.* New York: Alfred A. Knopf, 2005.

Danquah, Meri Nana-Ama. *Willow Weep for Me: A Black Woman's Journey Through Depression*. New York: W. W. Norton, 1998.

Fanon, Frantz. *The Wretched of the Earth*. New York: Grove Weidenfeld Press, 1963.

Franklin, Mrs. Unpublished Manuscript. *Diary 1899–1907*. Duke University Special Collections Library. 2nd 64:B Box 6 (Small American Volumes).

Gary, Lawrence E. Ed. *Mental Health: A Challenge to the Black Community*. Philadelphia: Dorrance and Co., 1978.

Harris, Sylvia, with Eunetta T. Boone and William H. Boulware. *Long Shot: My Bipolar Life and the Horses Who Saved Me*. New York: Ecco Press, 2011.

Head, John. *Standing in the Shadows: Understanding and Overcoming Depression in Black Men*. New York: Broadway Books, 2004.

June, Lee N., and Sabrina D. Black. *Counseling in African-American Communities: Biblical Perspectives on Tough Issues*. Grand Rapids, MI: Zondervan, 2002.

Karp, David A. *Speaking of Sadness: Depression, Disconnection, and the Meanings of Illness*. New York: Oxford University Press, 1996.

Lerner, Barbara. *Therapy in the Ghetto: Political Impotence and Personal Disintegration*. Baltimore: Johns Hopkins University Press, 1972.

Ndegwa, David, and Dele Olajide. *Main Issues in Mental Health and Race*. Hants, UK: Ashgate Publishing, 2003.

Parker, Seymour, and Robert J. Kleiner. *Mental Illness in the Urban Negro Community*. New York: Free Press, 1996.

Poussaint, Alvin F., MD, and Amy Alexander. *Lay My Burden Down: Suicide and the Mental Health Crisis among African-Americans*. Boston: Beacon Press, 2000.

Roberts, J. D., MD. *Insanity in the Colored Race*. 1883. Duke University Special Collections Library. E Pam 12mo #9574.

Sager, Clifford J., MD, Thomas L. Brayboy, MD, and Barbara R. Waxenberg. *Family in Therapy: A Laboratory Experience*. New York: Grove Press, 1970.

Thomas, Alexander, MD, and Samuel Sillen, PhD. *Racism and Psychiatry*. New York: Brunner/Mazel Publishers, 1972.

Turner, Samuel M., and Russell T. Jones. *Behavior Modification in Black Populations: Psychosocial Issues and Empirical Findings*. New York: Plenum Press, 1982.

Selected Articles

Carney, S. M., and G. M. Goodwin. "Lithium—A Continuing Story in the Treatment of Bipolar Disorder." *Acta Psychiatrica Scandinavica* 111, no S426 (2005): 7–12.

Curtis, Vivienne A., Jim van Os, and Robin M. Murray. "The Kraepelinian Dichotomy: Evidence from Developmental and Neuroimaging Studies." *Journal of Neuropsychiatry and Clinical Neurosciences* 12, no.3 (Summer 2000): 398–405.

Decker, Hannah S. "The Psychiatric Works of Emil Kraepelin: A Many-Faceted Story of Modern Medicine." *Journal of the History of the Neuroscience*s 13, no. 3 (September 2004): 248–76.

Delbello, Melissa O., Cesar A. Soutullo, and Stephen M. Strakowski. "Racial Differences in Treatment of Adolescents with Bipolar Disorder." *American Journal of Psychiatry* 157, no. 5 (May 2000): 837–38.

Doss, Janet. "Coping with Depression: African American Perspective." *Journal of the American Psychiatric Nurses Association* 10, no. 5 (October 2004): 254–55.

Engels, Huub, Frank Heynick, and Cees van der Staak. "Emil Kraepelin's Dream Speech: A Psychoanalyic Interpretation." *International Journal of Psychoanalysis* 84, no. 5 (October 2003): 1281–94.

Fleck, David E., Wendi L. Hendricks, Melissa P. DelBello, and Stephen M. Strakowski. "Differential Prescription of Maintenance Antipsychotics to African American and White Patients with New-Onset Bipolar Disorder." *Journal of Clinical Psychiatry* 63, no. 8 (August 2002): 658–64.

Fleck, David E., and Stephen M. Strakowski. "Differential Prescription of Maintenance Antipsychotics to African American and White Patients with New-Onset Bipolar Disorder: Drs. Fleck and Strakowski Reply." *Journal of Clinical Psychiatry* 64, no. 5 (May 2003): 615.

Guarnaccia, Peter J., and Pilar Parra. "Ethnicity, Social Status and Families' Experiences of Caring for a Mentally Ill Family Member." *Community Mental Health Journal* 32, no. 3 (June 1996): 243–60.

Jacob, Joseph Simeon. "A Comparative Study of the Incidence of Insanity Among Negroes and Whites." *Bulletin of the University of Georgia* 38, no. 2a (February 1938), published in *Georgia University Phelps-Stokes Fellowship Studies* 14.

Kilbourne, Amy M., Gretchen L. Hass, Benoit H. Mulsant, Mark S. Bauer, and Harold A. Pincus. "Concurrent Psychiatric Diagnoses by Age and Race Among Persons with Bipolar Disorder." *Psychiatric Services* 55, no. 8 (August 2004): 931–33.

Kupfer, David J., Ellen Frank, Victoria J. Grochocinski, Patricia R. Houck, and Charlotte Brown. "African-American Participants in a Bipolar Disorder Registry: Clinical and Treatment Characteristics." *Bipolar Disorders* 7, no. 1 (February 2005): 82–88.

Lewis, Dorothy Otnow, MD, David A. Balla, PhD, and Shelley S. Shanok, MPH. "Some Evidence of Race Bias in the Diagnosis and Treatment of the Juvenile Offender." *American Journal of Orthopsychiatry* 49, no. 1 (January 1979): 53–61.

Maggini, Carlo, Paola Salvatore, Angela Gerhard, and Paolo Migone. "Psychopathology of Stable and Unstable Mixed States: A Historical View." *Comprehensive Psychiatry* 41, no. 2 (March–April 2000): 77–82.

Marneros, Andreas. "Bipolarity from Ancient to Modern Times: Conception, Birth and Rebirth." *Journal of Affective Disorders* 67, no. 1–3 (December 2001): 3–19.

———. "Expanding the Group of Bipolar Disorders." *Journal of Affective Disorders* 62, no.1–2 (January 2001): 39–44.

———."Origin and Development of Concepts of Bipolar Mixed States." *Journal of Affective Disorders* 67, no. 1–3 (December 2001): 229–40.

Moller, H. "Is Lithium Still the Gold Standard in the Treatment of Bipolar Disorders?" *European Archives of Psychiatry and Clinical Neuroscience* 253, no. 113 (June 2003): 113–14.

Mondimore, Francis M. "Kraepelin and Manic-Depressive Insantiy: An Historical Perspective." *International Review of Psychiatry* 17, no. 1 (February 2005): 49–52.

Morrison, Eileen F., and Karen A. Thornton. "Influence of Southern Spiritual Beliefs on Perceptions of Mental Illness." *Issues in Mental Health Nursing* 20, no. 5 (September–October 1999): 443–58.

Neighbors, Harold W., Steven J. Trierweiler, Briggett C. Ford, and Jordana R. Muroff. "Racial Differences in DSM Diagnosis Using a Semi-Structured Instrument: The Importance of Clinical Judgment in the Diagnosis of African Americans." *Journal of Health and Social Behavior* 44, no. 3 (September 2003): 237–56.

Oyserman, Daphna, Deborah Bybee, Carol T. Mowbray, and Peter McFarlane. "Positive Parenting among African American Mothers with a Serious Mental Illness." *Journal of Marriage and Family* 64, no. 1 (February 2002): 65–77.

Pollack, Linda E., Sheila Harvin, and Roxy D. Cramer. "Coping Resources of African-American and White Patients Hospitalized for Bipolar Disorder." *Psychiatric Services* 51, no. 10 (October 2000): 1310–2.

Shenk, Joshua Wolf. "Lincoln's Great Depression." *Atlantic Monthly* 296, no. 3 (October 2005): 52–62.

Simoneau, Teresa L., David Miklowitz, Jeffrey A. Richards, Rakhshanda Saleem, and Elizabeth L. George. "Bipolar Disorder and Family Communication: Effects of a Psychoeducational Treatment Program." *Journal of Abnormal Psychology* 108, no. 4 (April 1999): 588–97.

Strakowski, Stephen M., Susan L. McElroy, Paul E. Keck Jr., and Scott A. West. "Racial Influence on Diagnosis in Psychotic Mania." *Journal of Affective Disorders* 39, no. 2 (July 1996): 157–62.

Szarek, Bonnie L., and John W. Goethe. "Racial Differences in Use of Antipsychotics Among Patients with Bipolar Disorder." *Journal of Clinical Psychiatry* 64, no. 5 (May 2003): 614–5.

Trede, Katharina, Paola Salvatore, Christopher Baethge, Angela Gerhard, Carlo Maggini, Ross Baldessarini. "Manic-Depressive

Illness: Evolution in Kraepelin's Textbook, 1883–1926." *Harvard Review of Psychiatry* 13, no. 3 (May–June 2005): 155–78.

Whaley, Arthur L. "Ethnicity/Race, Paranoia, and Hospitalization for Mental Health Problems Among Men." *American Journal of Public Health* 94, no. 1 (January 2004): 78–81.

Wyman, Rufus. "A Discourse on Mental Philosophy as Connected with Mental Disease, Delivered before the Massachusetts Medical Society, 1830." In *Three Hundred Years of Psychiatry, 1535–1860: A History Presented in Selected English Texts*, edited by Richard Hunter and Ida Macalpine, 810–11. London: Oxford University Press, 1963.

Selected Websites

- **Active Minds**: www.activeminds.org
  This is an organization featuring the student voice in the conversation about mental health on college campuses. Chapters exist on campuses across the United States.

- **American Residential Treatment Association**: www.artausa.org
  This website catalogues information about mental health facilities available for people with mental health issues.

- **Bipolar Caregivers**: www.bipolarcaregivers.org
  This website lists resources for caregivers of people with bipolar disorder.

- **The Brain and Behavior Research Foundation**: www.narsad.org
  The Brain and Behavior Research Foundation (formerly NARSAD, the National Alliance for Research on Schizophrenia

and Depression) is committed to alleviating the suffering of those with mental illness by awarding grants that will lead to advances and breakthroughs in scientific research.

- **Bring Change 2 Mind**: www.bringchange2mind.org
  This is a nonprofit organization, endorsed by celebrity supporters, whose mission is to fight the stigma associated with mental illness.

- **Depression and Bipolar Support Alliance**: www.dbsalliance.org
  This organization aims to provide hope, help, and support to improve the lives of people living with mood disorders. DBSA pursues and accomplishes this mission through peer-based, recovery-oriented, empowering services and resources offered when people want them, where they want them, and how they want to receive them. Their website also offers useful suggestions for caregivers.

- **Dual Recovery Anonymous**: www.draonline.org
  Dual Recovery Anonymous is an independent, nonprofessional, twelve-step, self-help membership organization for people with dual diagnoses. Their website provides information about existing resource centers.

- **International Bipolar Foundation**: www.internationalbipolar-foundation.org
  This organization hopes to eliminate bipolar disorder through the advancement of research, promote and enhance care and support services for those affected by bipolar disorder, and erase stigma about mental illness through public education. Their website offers suggestions for caregivers.

- **Juvenile Bipolar Research Foundation**: www.jbrf.org
  The Juvenile Bipolar Research Foundation is the first charitable organization dedicated solely to the support of research for the study of early-onset bipolar disorder.

- **Metro Atlanta Recovery Residences (MARR)**: www.marrinc.org
  MARR is a private, nonprofit organization providing long-term residential treatment for men and women affected by chemical dependency. The facility offers recovery programs for both men and women.

- **Mental Health America**: www.mentalhealthamerica.net
  This nonprofit organization addresses all aspects of mental health and mental illness. Their website offers information on mental health advocacy and includes a list of frequently asked questions about mental illness.

- **National Alliance on Mental Illness (NAMI)**: www.nami.org
  NAMI is a grassroots mental health advocacy organization that focuses on educating America about mental illness. Their website provides descriptions of all mental illnesses.

- **National Suicide Prevention Lifeline**: www.suicideprevention-lifeline.org
  The National Suicide Prevention Lifeline (800-273-8255) is a twenty-four-hour, toll-free, confidential suicide-prevention hotline available to anyone in suicidal crisis or emotional distress. Their website provides support for caregivers, family, and friends.

- **Pendulum**: www.pendulum.org
  This website provides information, support, and education related to bipolar disorder and depression.

- **Skyland Trail**: www.skylandtrail.org
  Skyland Trail offers varied programs and services, including residential and day treatment, primary care, support groups, and vocational counseling, to people living with mental illness. The facility is nonprofit and provides community-based services. Future plans include a specialized program for young adults.

- **Substance Abuse and Mental Health Services Administration (SAMHSA)**: www.samhsa.gov
  The mission of this governmental agency is to reduce the impact of substance abuse and mental illness on America's communities.

- **Treatment Advocacy Center (TAC)**: www.treatmentadvocacy-center.org
  This national nonprofit organization is dedicated to eliminating barriers to the timely and effective treatment of severe mental illness. They advocate for new laws pertaining to the lives of those with mental illness.

SERENITY PRAYER

God, grant me the serenity to accept the things I cannot change,
courage to change the things I can,
And wisdom to know the difference.

—Reinhold Niebuhr

index